For

Chris Boardman MBE

Ron 'Swasie' Turner is an extrovert and a 'character' to say the least. His life could, perhaps, be described as having been rich and full, but also tragic.

However, 'Swasie' has always 'ploughed his own furrow' and dealt with everything that life has thrown at him with amazing energy, commitment and drive.

This is the fourth book he has tackled since 1994 and it, like its predecessors, helps to illustrate how he has dealt with life's blows in a positive and productive way.

So why am I writing this foreword and what is it that 'Swasie' and I have in common?

Well, for starters we both live on the Wirral peninsula a place, for all its faults, we both call home.

We both spend most of our time on wheels too, and have both raced around the TT circuit of the Isle of Man!

We are both of us, if the truth be told, stubborn buggers who aren't very good at accepting advice!

And lastly, I suspect that we both hold with the same philosophy that "Life is messy! You can choose to see that as a problem, or you can choose to see that as a challenge!"

Which point of view have you chosen?

With my best wishes for your future insane endeavours!

Chris Boardman MBE
World & Olympic Cycling Champion

To Keith & Sue with
my compliments & sincere
best Wishes

from

Swasie

Fri April 20th 2001

**This book is dedicated
to the memory of
Marje Turner**

1

Sergeant R Swasie Turner prepares to lay a wreath on behalf of Merseyside Police at Wallasey War Memorial during the Remembrance Day Parade and Service in November 1986

Ronald 'Swasie' Turner –

'Wheelchair Pilot'

'Swasie' Turner is a man of many parts, a man of hidden depths and latent talents.

Swasie is, also, a man who wears his 'heart on his sleeve' and he always has. He is one in that great British tradition of 'larger than life characters', extrovertly personified by his trademark 'handlebar' moustache, which he has sported since his late teens, together with a military and upright bearing from his many years in the services.

> **one in that great British tradition of 'larger than life characters'...**

> **you earn respect from your words and your actions, not from a few 'pips' on your shoulder...**

He has actually seen duty in three different services, the Territorial Army, the Fire Service and the Police Force, and to all of them he has brought his own style and his own personality. At times abrasive, at others highly supportive of less confident colleagues, Swasie has always stood up for the 'little man', whether physically small, without a voice or without the clout of rank or status.

Throughout his career, but particularly during his later years in the police force, his outspoken no-nonsense attitude clearly limited promotional prospects, but Swasie has never been one to worry about rank or officialdom.

As far as he is concerned you earn respect from your words and your actions, not from a few 'pips' on your shoulder or the size of your car or office.

He has been, at times, a stern taskmaster to junior ranks always demanding the best, but he has always been fair and has stood shoulder to shoulder with them when they needed support. He has never shirked from telling his 'superiors' a few home truths when he thought they were deserved. His sheer power of personality coupled with the strength and presence of his super-fit physical frame has always ensured that he would get his point of view over, whether appreciated or not.

Among Swasie's lesser known attributes, however, is an artistic talent, belying his physique, which stretches from pen and ink to the sophistication of oil and watercolour painting. When this talent was coupled with his sometimes wicked sense of humour it resulted in a series of cartoons. These were produced throughout his many years in the police force. Most of them were strictly for internal amusement within the force itself where, on the station notice board, he would parody insensitive or officious senior ranks or mock red-tape and petty restrictions.

But, all the cartoons would be signed with his own distinctive 'Swasie' signature. Many of his cartoons, though, were of a much broader interest and some of them are reproduced here in the following pages.

Over recent years, and particularly since his enforced 'early retirement' from the service which was his life, Swasie has also turned his talents, energy

Swasie is never afraid to strongly speak his mind on subjects or personalities with whom he takes issue.

and enthusiasm to writing.

His first book entitled "Off the Cuff", an autobiography, was published in 1994 to be followed by a second in 1996, "If the Cap Fits", a novel about police life in Liverpool. Both have been huge successes and his third book, "Onto the Final Leg"

has also recently been published.

However, his literary output is not restricted just to books. He now regularly contributes to several publications including newspapers and magazines.

His monthly column in the local community magazine, Wirral Champion, has made him a popular and well-known personality on the peninsula. His outspoken views and opinions powerfully voice the concerns of many readers and those who are largely without a voice. Never afraid to strongly speak his mind on subjects or personalities with

“ ... his outspoken views and opinions voice the concerns of many of the readers... ”

"....the eccentric, outspoken, handlebar moustached ex-policeman is the personification of everything 'British'..."

whom he takes issue, Swasie is always interesting, always contraversial and always an editorial challenge!

His regular columns in Police Guardian, Police News, Brigade Guardian and Fire News, the newspapers of the police force and the fire service, put him in direct contact with most of the personnel working in these two great public services, and through his own direct experience he has adopted the mantle of 'spokesman' for many of their concerns.

Swasie, though, does not limit his literary efforts to these islands alone. He is

"...illustrates many amazing and almost unbelievable endeavours..."

also a regular contributor to the American Police Beat. Known as 'The Voice of the Nation's Law Enforcement Community', this is the newspaper serving the Police Forces of the United States of America, to whose perceptive readers the eccentric, outspoken, handlebar moustached ex-policeman is the personification of everything 'British'.

In yet another field, Swasie's growing 'notoriety' together with his outspoken views have made him a sought-after speaker at meetings of organisations as varied as local schools, businessmen's clubs, from ladies' guilds and institutes to debating societies and writers' clubs.

This book has several themes;

1. It is a brief chronicle of his life and an explanation of his commitment to fund-raising.

2. It is a compendium of many of the articles he has had published in magazines and newspapers on subjects wide and diverse.

3. It is a showcase for some of his paintings and

cartoons.

4. But, most of all, it describes in detail and graphically illustrates many of the amazing and almost unbelievable endeavours he has undertaken over the last few years raising funds for 'his pet charity' the Clatterbridge Cancer Gene Appeal in memory of his late and beloved wife Marje.

Swasie Turner - policeman, soldier, fireman, author, artist, critic, campaigner, cartoonist, spokesman, speaker, fund-raiser, fighter, character - but above all - a true Champion.

Swasie is a Champion of so many things;

He is the People's Champion.

He is the Police Force Champion.

He is the Fire Service Champion.

But, above all else he is a Charity's Champion - The Clatterbridge Cancer Gene Appeal.

Read on and be amazed and humbled and, if you're like me, be moved.......

J.M.Birtwistle

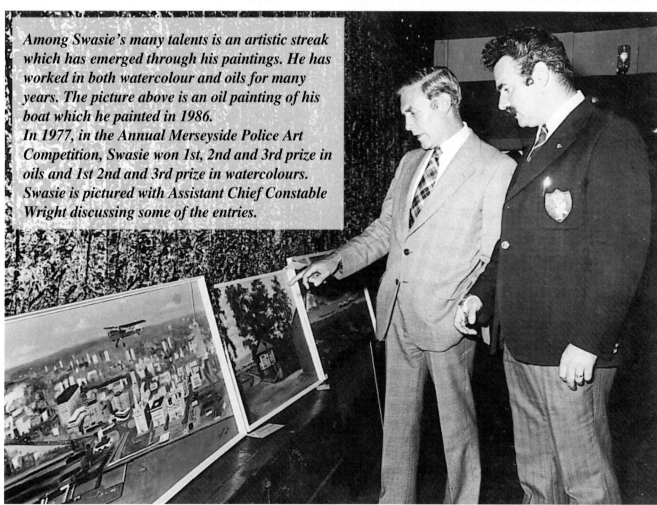

Among Swasie's many talents is an artistic streak which has emerged through his paintings. He has worked in both watercolour and oils for many years. The picture above is an oil painting of his boat which he painted in 1986.

In 1977, in the Annual Merseyside Police Art Competition, Swasie won 1st, 2nd and 3rd prize in oils and 1st 2nd and 3rd prize in watercolours. Swasie is pictured with Assistant Chief Constable Wright discussing some of the entries.

Contents

*above, Swasie, standing in the doorway,
with fellow firemen at Heswall Fire Station
in 1962 and, below, 'larking about' at the
fire brigade special training course held at
Morton-in-the-Marsh in 1963*

*above, Swasie and Marje at
the Police Academy in
Bruche, Warrington, after
he passed out and started
his police career*

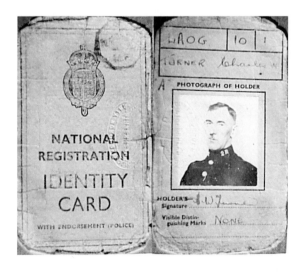

*both Swasie's grandfather, above,
Sergeant George Woods, and his uncle, left, Constable
William Charles Turner, had served in Birkenhead Police*

Ronald 'Swasie' Turner

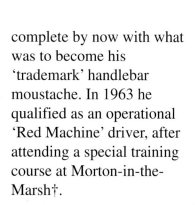

complete by now with what was to become his 'trademark' handlebar moustache

'Swasie' Turner was born in Saughall Massie, Wirral, in 1940 and has spent his entire life on the peninsula.

After schooling at Overchurch Primary and Prenton Secondary, Swasie joined the Territorial Army where he served for 3½ years. It was during this time, in 1958, that he married his long-time sweetheart, Marjorie Pringle of Hoylake.

In 1961, however, frustrated at being turned down by the police force, he joined the Cheshire County Fire Brigade as Fireman 1633,

complete by now with what was to become his 'trademark' handlebar moustache. In 1963 he qualified as an operational 'Red Machine' driver, after attending a special training course at Morton-in-the-Marsh†.

During four years in the brigade Fireman Turner attended numerous

incidents, many serious, some, sadly, fatal, and on many occasions he rescued casualties from burning premises with little thought for his own safety.

Swasie also became well known in the brigade, not only for his moustache and extrovert personality but also for his prowess with the infamous hook ladder††.

---

† *Morton-in-the-Marsh - This Home Office Training Establishment had been a wartime RAF air base made famous on BBC Radio in the late 40s by Richard Murdoch, Kenneth Horne and Sam Costa. They served there together during the war and their popular radio show fictitiously named after it was the popular, "Much-Binding-in-the-Marsh".*

†† *The hook ladder was a device developed in the 60s to deal with fires in the new multi-storey blocks of flats which were then being built. It consisted of a relatively short ladder with a large hook on the top which could be 'hooked' onto the window ledge above allowing the fireman to climb up and onto the ledge. It would then be*

moved up to the next storey and so on permitting the fireman to reach heights considerably in excess of the available machine-mounted ladders of the time. Needless to say, it took a certain kind of fireman to face the challenge - after all there was no safety net or safety line - Swasie, however, was just that kind of fireman!

Since his enforced retirement, Swasie has developed , many of his talents, not least of which has been his ability to talk! He is now a much sought after-dinner speaker

However, by this time, 1965, Swasie was determined that his true vocation was with that other service - the police force. He very much wanted to follow in the footsteps of many of his family including his grandfather and uncle, both of whom had been policemen. So it was that, after serving some time as a Special Constable and then as a Parks Policeman, Swasie's determination finally paid off and he was accepted into Liverpool City Police.

After an initial training period at the National Police Academy in Bruche, near Warrington, Swasie passed out and started his career as a constable.

His 'apprenticeship' commenced at the 'sharp end' in Rose Hill Bridewell, the police station known universally as 'Spike

Island'. His beat covered the notorious Scotland Road area and included much of Liverpool's tough downtown dockland.

Later, he was selected to become one of Bert Balmer's famous 'Commandos'. Bert Balmer was then the Chief Constable of Liverpool and his 'Commandos' were specially chosen police officers posing in plain clothes as newspaper sellers, street sweepers and many other unobtrusive roles.

An enthusiastic young bobby, Swasie eventually aspired to the ranks of the CID. Here he spent some

time with the Metropolitan Police down at Scotland Yard where he was, supposedly, trained to be a better 'sleuth'. In later years he was also to serve for some time in the Vice Squad.

Eventually, though, after a number of years in 'civvies', he returned to his colleagues in blue - the uniformed ranks.

In the mid 70s Swasie was selected for special firearms training and, as such, performed many operational duties, particularly during the intense period of IRA activity in Liverpool during which two of his colleagues

"Swasie's determination finally paid off and he was accepted into Liverpool City Police..."

were shot down and seriously injured.

With his fine physique and extrovert personality, Swasie had always been a keen boxer and also an enthusiastic weightlifter. In the police service he found he was able to maintain this fitness by regular workouts in the force's gyms. He also assisted in the running of a boxing club in the inner city's notorious Toxteth area. During this period of service in Liverpool he devoted much of his spare time and energy to the youths of the Myrtle Gardens Boxing Club.

Some time later whilst serving at Liverpool's Copperas Hill station, Constable Turner was promoted to Sergeant. Then, a year later, he was

Swasie on duty at New Brighton during Power Boat day in the summer of 1986

> *"he was awarded the Shipwreck & Humane Society's Certificate for saving the life of a man collapsed in the street"*

transferred 'across the water', and nearer home, to Wallasey on Wirral.

Shortly after arriving at Wallasey, at a ceremony in the Town Hall, he was awarded the Shipwreck & Humane Society's Certificate for saving the life of a gentleman who had collapsed in Dale Street, Liverpool. Swasie had resuscitated him twice whilst awaiting the ambulance service though, sadly, the gentleman, a local magistrate, died shortly after in hospital. Some time later Swasie was also awarded the Police Long Service Medal.

However, it was here in Wallasey that Swasie's police career was to be brought to a dramatic and premature end. Whilst on duty in New Brighton he attempted to stop a speeding motorcyclist on a high powered Kawasaki when he

Swasie in typical pose in one of his favourite vehicles - Land Rover NKB 716 M on patrol in the 70s from Westminster Road Station

Swasie has always enjoyed the sea and sailing - he is pictured here at Dee Sailing Club in 1990

was deliberately knocked down. He received severe injuries to the right side of his body but particularly to his right leg and knee which were very badly broken, damaged and shattered.

Over the following years he was to undergo no less than 14 separate operations on this severely damaged leg including two knee replacements. It gradually became clear, however, that he would never be able to return to active service and he eventually bowed to the inevitable, and, in 1990, was invalided from the job that had been his vocation and his life.

During this very traumatic period fate also struck Marje, his beloved wife of nearly forty years. Marje, who he had known since they were both 15, had been diagnosed as having a cancerous lump in her breast. However, the operation had appeared to

be a success and with constant medication and treatment her cancer went into remission.

Unfortunately, though, Swasie's own problems were not improving and, sadly, in November 1996, his right leg, which was not responding satisfactorily to all the surgery, had to be amputated above the knee.

The effect on Swasie - a man of considerable energy and physique, a rumbustious 'no-nonsense' all action copper - a boxer, a weightlifter, an athlete - can hardly be imagined.

Swasie was known in Wallasey for 'walking the legs off' his constables

when out on the beat. However, with Marje, his 'pillar of strength' at his side, Swasie reluctantly accepted his situation and quickly adapted to the challenge of this new life in a wheelchair.

Now, devoid of the job he loved, of the work he enjoyed and the problems which absorbed his mind, Swasie needed a challenge! He quickly found the outlet and turned his boundless energies to raising funds to help fight that dreaded disease, cancer - the disease which had recently so nearly claimed his beloved wife, Marje.

In his standard issue DHS wheelchair, a veritable 'tank' weighing in at 57 lbs, and strongly against medical advice, he set about travelling huge distances. But, as throughout his whole life, Swasie had never been one to take advice! He wanted, above all, to raise money for the Clatterbridge Cancer Gene Appeal and, come hell or high water, he was going to.

Clatterbridge, the northwest's leading centre for oncology, was the hospital that had cared for Marje during her own

it gradually became clear, however, that he would never return to active service...

"Swasie threw himself totally into what was now his life's obsession..."

traumatic experience and so Swasie set about doing as much as he could to assist in the fight against this horrendous disease.

All seemed to be going smoothly until late in 1997, just one year after the amputation of his right leg. Tragically, and with sudden and deadly consequences, Marje's cancer reappeared. Within the short period of just five weeks Marje had died leaving a totally broken and inconsolable Swasie.

Unable, to this day, to come to terms with the loss of his lifelong sweetheart and best friend, Swasie threw himself totally into what was now to become his life's obsession. His one aim from now on was to raise as much money as possible, by any eccentric or unusual means, in his quest to fight the killer disease that had robbed him of his beloved wife Marje.

Swasie has done, and will continue to do, anything that has never before been done in a wheelchair. The harder and seemingly more impossible the challenge, the more eccentric the

Swasie was awarded the Shipwreck & Humane Society's Certificate, at a ceremony in the Town Hall, for saving the life of a man who had collapsed in Dale Street, Liverpool

endeavour, the more determined is Swasie to successfully complete the venture, whatever it is.

Consequently, not only has our 'wheelchair pilot' broken new ground, which he hopes will be inspirational to others in a similar position, but he has set new records of sheer physical endurance. At the same time he has raised considerable sums of money for his charity, the Clatterbridge Cancer Gene Appeal, in memory of Marje.

Distance and inclement weather have long since

ceased to be a concern. Swasie's powerful arms and upper body strength propel his DHS castored wheelchair between 15 and 20 plus miles daily achieving total distances that the wheelchair manufacturer can only wonder at.

Over 4,500 miles in just two years, on roads, mountain tracks, beaches, up stairs and ladders and across muddy fields, is testament to Swasie's commitment to his cause as well as to the strength of his 'trusty steed'.

J. M. Birtwistle

13

Swasie Turner ..... Off The Cuff

PTSS Compensation?

I wonder if the results and findings of the Hillsborough tragedy will ever reach a satisfactory conclusion?
My deep and sincere sympathy goes out to *all* those families who lost loved ones, and I hope one day perhaps, financial compensation will come their way to help alleviate, in some way, the trauma they have all suffered.

Wirral Champion – April 1997
This was Swasie's first column for Wirral Champion Magazine. He had been invited by the editor, John M Birtwistle, to contribute to the magazine after much 'lobbying' and persistence by Swasie - qualities which were to serve him well over the next few years...

However my sentiments do *not* extend to those of my ex-colleagues who were awarded obscene sums by way of compensation for their "Post Traumatic Stress Syndrome" due to what those few successful claimant officers saw on that day. Yes, the whole tragic scenario was

'Black Beauty' was painted in oils by Swasie in 1986 for a very old friend of the family

WIRRAL Champion
magazine

The original free courtesy magazine

> **"...my sentiments do not extend to those ex-colleagues awarded obscene sums of compensation..."**

indeed 'traumatic'. But, are we not, as police officers, and as members of the emergency services, thoroughly trained to face and deal with such very incidents? What about the *untrained, civilian* throngs who left the terraces to tend the injured and assist in any way that they could? What about the ambulance crews, nurses, and doctors?

What about the countless times that fire fighters have to bring out the charred remains, including women and children, from house fires, or cut their bloody remains from wrecked

vehicles? I haven't heard any of those equally stressed men and women bleating, and receiving huge sums of money to compensate for *their* stress!

Before anyone asks do *I* know the meaning of PTSS? - *YES!* - I can assure you I do. I, too, was once a fireman involved in

such cases before becoming a "front line" bobby.

For over a quarter of a century I saw service in which, injury wise, "I've had my moments!" I wouldn't hesitate to go through it all again, though, such is my dedication to "the cloth". However, like those other members of the emergency services, I thought that's what we were there for, and I got on with it.

I bet you there are a number of CICB (Criminal Injuries Compensation Board) claimants amongst local bobbies who have suffered or *are* suffering far worse *and have received far less!*

I rest my case!

Swasie Turner

> **"are we not, as police officers, trained to face and deal with such very incidents?"**

The Ascent of Leasowe Lighthouse

Monday 7th July 1997

The ascent of Leasowe Lighthouse on the North Wirral coast, not far from Swasie's home in Upton, was his first major 'exploit' to be given widespread publicity. The concept of a 'climb' being carried out from a wheelchair, or more correctly, with a wheelchair, was quite unique.

An amazing and unique event took place at Leasowe Lighthouse on Monday 7th July 1997.

Swasie Turner climbed to the top of Leasowe lighthouse to highlight the work of the Friends of Leasowe Lighthouse*.

This group's efforts have enabled the historic building to be open to the public.

Swasie managed to negotiate the 130 steps of the narrow spiral staircase rising to over 100 feet. That in itself was a remarkable feat for a disabled person, however, what made it quite unique was that Swasie took his wheelchair with him!

At first Swasie, himself, was somewhat apprehensive of what he had let himself in for. But Swasie is a trier, and once he said he'd do it, then do it he would!

The wheelchair, by the way, is not one of those lightweight trikes that you see the racers in the London Marathon tearing round in. No, it is a standard issue NHS heavyweight - built to last - not built for speed, and certainly not for carting up 130 steps! Thanks to his many years of weight-lifting and his now regular roadwork and cross-country wheelchair mileage, Swasie was able to tackle this seemingly impossible task.

There to oversee this 'event' were Adam King and Mike Garbutt of the Wirral Countryside Rangers. Swasie admitted afterwards that the climb was an effort! However, he was at pains to point out that he was at all times completely unaided, confirmed by the Rangers.

Once at the top, Swasie looked out on a view never seen before from a wheelchair! In over two hundred years no-one has ever sat at the top of the lighthouse in a wheelchair. It seems certain to remain a unique achievement!

*The Friends of Leasowe Lighthouse produce a newsletter and hold Open Days at the lighthouse which the oldest brick built lighthouse still standing in the British Isles. They provide visitors with the information they need to understand the maritime history of Wirral. Enquiries may be made to the Chairman on 0151 678 6828 or the Secretary on 0151 677 1228 or to the Rangers at the lighthouse on 0151 678 5488. The lighthouse is open to the public on the 1st and 3rd Sunday each month from 1pm to 4pm.

> *"what made it quite unique was that Swasie took his wheelchair with him...."*

*above, Swasie pauses for breath, on
the stairs to the Ranger's Office,
wondering what he has taken on!
But all is well as, below, Swasie
admires the view from the top of
Leasowe lighthouse, accompanied
by TV cameraman, Ally Boxie*

*Swasie sits outside the
famous lighthouse after his
historic climb and enjoys
the warm sunshine*

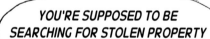

Swasie's cartoons touched on a variety of topics within the police force. This selection includes one, above, which, prophetically, preceded the serious accident involving a motorcycle which, ultimately, ended his police career

Swasie Turner ..... Off The Cuff

'On the Square'

Wirral Champion – May 1997

Swasie's second column for Wirral Champion Magazine tackled a subject which was causing some concern not only in the press, but also in Parliament itself....

Why on earth do those in the police service who are 'on the square' (ie; as members of a Masonic Lodge) dither so much about saying so?
You're not doing any wrong by being such, *are you?* Masonry in its entirety is *totally* charitable and honourable in its untiring contributions to many deserving and needy causes, of that there is *no* doubt.

Why then, the reluctance to "cough" if asked? Granted, it's nobody's business, and it's not as though those officers who are Masons would be expected to go out on patrol with their trouser leg rolled up and their chest left bare! Anyway, why single out the police service when suggesting that membership of a Lodge could cloud one's vision of impartiality. What about judges? Oh, yes, many members of the judiciary are devout members of the Lodge, as are prison officers, solicitors, barristers, doctors and vicars ... the list of those who could be "biased" is endless. For goodness sake, if those whinging, moaning, holier than thou hypocrites want something to whine about, ... *tell them!* There's nothing wrong with being a genuine Mason so long as no conflicts of loyalty or interest are allowed to manifest themselves, as only then would criticism be justified.

So, if you are not in anyway compromised by your off duty activities, *cough!,* and shut up all those whingers in their ignorance once and for all.

Last month in my article about Hillsborough I was talking about nurses and doctors. In conclusion, I would like to draw maximum attention to those in the profession who regularly patch us up after those angry, violent members of our society have so often "vented their spleen" and inflicted numerous injuries on us.

They are *always* there when we need them. I'm sure I speak for everybody when I say a **BIG, BIG** thank you to those very doctors and nurses who have tended and mended us.

God bless you all, we'd be lost without you, you grossly overworked and underpaid angels.

Swasie Turner

> "*Masonry is totally charitable and honourable in its contributions to many deserving causes...*"

above, Swasie pauses during his struggle up the narrow spiral staircase

main picture, Swasie approaches the lighthouse across New Brighton beach

below, Relieved to reach the top and to enjoy the superb view from the balcony

"he made his way across the obstacle course of the rock strewn shore...."

Ascent of New Brighton Lighthouse

On a hot Friday in August, with the sun burning down from a cloudless sky, Swasie made his way from the shadow of Fort Perch Rock.

He was setting out from Wallasey's historic landmark to scale yet another lighthouse.

This time it was New Brighton lighthouse. A crowd had gathered with a TV crew in attendance as Swasie made his way across the obstacle course of the rock strewn shore that would have been difficult for the able bodied let alone in a standard NHS wheelchair.

As he approached the lighthouse he hit a real obstacle in the 'moat' of muddy water which now surrounds this pillar of concrete. However, Swasie was adamant that he would accept no assistance from the watching Dougie Darrock, son David or the ex-fire brigade officer there to ensure his safety.

Leaving his mud-clogged wheelchair Swasie hopped through the water to the base of the lighthouse to the ladder which would take him to the entrance high up the side of the tower. Eventually with a great deal of effort, and several cuts and scratches, Swasie reached the doorway and sat recovering his breath before hauling up his wheelchair on the end of a long rope.

If that wasn't hard enough the next stage inside the tower was even more difficult. The narrow concrete spiral staircase was very steep and included two almost vertical timber

Fort Perch Rock in the foreground and the Liverpool skyline in the distance - the superb view from the balcony of the lighthouse

sections. Undaunted, Swasie set off up the stairs, grunting and shedding buckets of perspiration. Finally our one-legged crusader reached the top of the building, almost 100 feet above the sand. On the balcony, complete with wheelchair, Swasie took a welcome rest and enjoyed the warm applause of the watching crowd.

After a short respite, Swasie returned to mother earth by the same route, which was even more demanding. Emerging from the entrance in the side he lowered his trusty NHS 'steed' down into the water and eventually rejoined it for the return to relatively 'dry' land.

Following a short interview with the TV crew he was mobbed by well-wishers who donated generously to his Cancer Gene Appeal.

The ascent of the lighthouse at New Brighton, which guards the entrance to the Mersey, was a natural progression after the success of his first 'climb', and, in such a prominent position, attracted a large 'audience'

21

Swasie Turner ..... Off The Cuff

'Zero Tolerance Policing'

I do not wish to patronise either politics or politicians, if I can help it!, but ...
Political parties apart, it sickens me (and no doubt thousands of other God fearing and law abiding citizens) when, every time the Home Secretary attempts to curb, deter or punish our fellow members of society who have absolutely no intention of adhering to our rules, and insist on assaulting, raping, or robbing us .... out of the woodwork crawl those ever whining, persistent 'do gooders'.

Wirral Champion - June 1997
By the time Swasie had started work on his third column for Wirral Champion Magazine he had already developed a reputation and a following. The editor decided that his previous limit of 350 words could be increased to 600 or so.... Swasie rose to the occasion with a hard hitting piece on a subject raising 'temperatures' across the country.....

These out of touch pacifists and persistent appeasers have had their say for the last twenty or thirty years, during which time our morals and self discipline have been eroded almost beyond redemption.

The 'do gooders' have continually undermined all efforts to restore law and order by the imposition of toughness. 'Discipline' and 'Respect' have become dirty words and the more the authorities try to enforce the laws of the land, for the benefit, security and protection of us all, squeals of 'Police brutality' are heard. The worse the crime, the more it is deemed by those pathetic protectors of our 'civil rights' that the wicked perpetrator of such atrocities is a ...

'misunderstood cry for help in the wilderness by one who has fallen from the plank of righteousness into the sea of evil, and has been swept away on the tide of nastiness and is therefore entitled to be anointed with the balm of human kindness'!

Obviously, if the victim had not been in the wrong place at the wrong time, or had not been 'provocatively'

> **the 'do gooders' have continually undermined all efforts to restore law and order by the imposition of toughness...**

dressed, or hadn't owned or possessed that which the deviant wanted for himself, he or she wouldn't have been robbed or raped, so it was partly the victim's fault!!!!

It has been established in the USA, and now here, that 'zero tolerance' policing works! ... but - is it right for the big, nasty policeman to be horrid and tough with pavement cyclists, car tax dodgers, violent bullies, child molesters, robbers, rapists and killers?

Again, according to the lily livered brigade of 'do gooders', No! We must turn the other cheek and 'show understanding' to these habitual wrong doers!

In Middlesborough, Cleveland, Chief Inspector Ray Mallon has taken the initiative, and in doing so he has upset a lot of 'sirs' in the comfort of their ivory

Sawsie and Ray Mallon had a lot in common to talk about when they met in 1997

> "Zero Tolerance is a liability which can lead to the upsetting of criminals...!"
>
> Chief Constable Thames Valley Police

towers by reducing Cleveland's crime figures and increasing the prison population, together with reuniting a large number of very distressed members of the public with their stolen property!

As the howls of protest emanate from the spineless 'do gooders', who should be applauding this very same plucky and courageous officer and his team. We now have ... would you 'Adam an Eve' it ... a bleating Chief Constable? Yes ... Chief Constable Charles Pollard of Thames Valley Police (a good force), branded zero tolerance as a "Liability which can lead to the upsetting of criminals and therefore a risk to public disorder". Many of our own Merseyside officers give their all to protect us, for which we should all be grateful (even though that is what they are paid for!), so

if and when a 'sir', in our own force adopts such tactics, (some already have, others have been doing it for years!) let us sincerely hope that our Chief Constable backs his troops all the way on this issue.

As well as zero tolerance thwarting society's deviants, we could do with weeding out those defeatists in the police who haven't got the 'bottle' to come out and show that they back the lads at the sharp end.

New York police chief's 'zero tolerance' strategy lowered their city's crime rate by 37%! Hartlepool's same tactics reduced reported crime by 27%, together with a massive 56% reduction in vehicle theft, plus a 31% reduction in burglary.

Any chance of Inspector Mallon transferring to Merseyside?

Swasie Turner

23

Swasie Turner .... At The Sharp End

Saturation Point of Public Tolerance

It is heart-warming to know that law abiding citizens have always been proud of their police service. Let us not forget, however, that the police function via 'public consent' and with their backing and assistance.

An example of selfless public spirit, was illustrated recently in Merseyside when a 19 year old student, Richard Thomas, and his father, disturbed a man breaking into a neighbour's house.

Police News – **November 1997**
By this time Swasie had been invited to write a column for the Police News - the independent national newspaper for the police forces of Britain. The editor had seen his work for Wirral Champion and was aware also of his first books. Swasie took the 'bull by the horns' and plunged into 'public tolerance' and support for the police.......

The dynamic duo tackled the offender and a violent struggle ensued during which a plate glass window was shattered injuring Richard's father and enabling the burglar to escape. He hadn't, however, appreciated young Richard's determination!

The student chased him for over a mile until he was apprehended with the help of a police officer. The offender has rightly, been jailed and Richard is to receive an award from the police for his heroism.

Although the service discourages vigilantes, it is little wonder that these groups spring up. Crime is spiralling out of control in this country whether those in authority admit it or not.

Recently another pillar of society, Mr Peter Spybey, reluctantly quit running a Neighbourhood Watch Scheme in Birmingham because he was let down by the police. His energetic and sometimes dangerous efforts to rid his estate of thieves, junkies and thugs were thwarted by lack of back up from his local force. On six occasions he

> **"Although the service discourages vigilantes, it is little wonder that these groups spring up..."**

Police News

No. 4   The National Newspaper for the Police Service   January 1999

> ## "Unfortunately, 'bottleless' mandarins in the force, and their political masters, are only concerned with status and image.."

requested assistance but police managed to turn up just ONCE!

Much as I am pro police, I have to agree that the 'cloth' has badly failed this lad.

Is it any wonder, then, when enterprising police officers try to stem this 'tide' of crime and anti social behaviour by initiative, using methods not deemed normal by some sirs, most give up in frustration.

Unfortunately, 'bottleless' mandarins in the force, and their political masters, are concerned only with status and image and are distant from the needs of the men and women who risk their lives.

Consequently, as happened recently in Bristol, the inevitable ensues....

A frustrated but enterprising Mr Andrew Burke formed a team of ex-soldiers to declare war on, to quote, *"Bristol's low life, criminal scum fraternity!"*

He says, *"We take the law to the extreme and tackle scumbags head on!"* Hmmm, sounds like a Ray Mallon in civvies? I just love Mr Burke's descriptive terminology and his sentiments.

Some 1,200 households in the Bristol area pay £1.35 per week for these services, which have resulted in a reduction of crime by 80 percent, though this is hotly disputed by Bristol police. But they would wouldn't they?

I personally, would pay such a fee if the results brought peace and security. But I am angry that a team of vigilantes should be receiving these accolades instead of the Police!

Cut backs and penny pinching are reducing public confidence in the efficiency of 'community policing' - so let's do something about it, NOW. Let's start by getting more uniforms out onto the streets where they belong!

> ## "...efforts to rid his estate of thieves, junkies and thugs were thwarted by lack of back up from his local force.."

The Great North 'Run'

14th September 1997

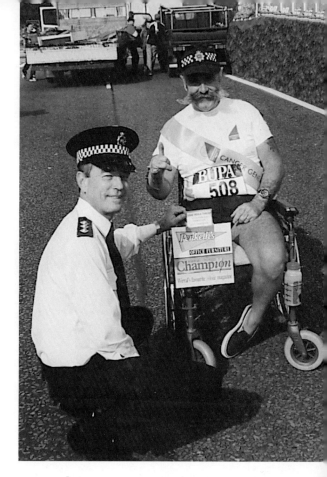

The Great North Run is held annually on Tyneside. This prestigious event in the athlete's calendar attracts household names. Runners from all over the world take part, as do top class international, wheelchair racers.

Their wheelchairs, though, are specially made for competitions, and weigh about 9lbs and incorporate brakes and steering.

These machines in the right hands can reach speeds of 35 miles per hour down even the slightest of gradients.

When Swasie applied to join the 1997 event, the powers that be were at first extremely reluctant to allow him entry. No such chair as his had to that time taken part, let alone completed the gruelling thirteen miles through Newcastle and beyond. It was not deemed possible that an ordinary DHS issue wheelchair could complete the distance due to its lack of roadworthy facilities, i.e. brakes and

above; Swasie is welcomed to Tyneside by Newastle's Chief Inspector Louis Hoareau who showed him the route

steering, and also its small castors as 'front wheels' - and it weighed a hefty 57lbs!

Not to be thwarted, the persistent Swasie continued to 'lobby' those reluctant authorities until he finally convinced them that he and his 'tank' could (and would!) complete the run.

Consequently those who were 'doubting Thomases' regarding Swasie's physical capabilities eventually allowed him to enter, although some still had reservations.

Swasie was there to raise funds for the Clatterbridge Cancer Gene Appeal, and was sponsored by Penketh's Stationers and Wirral Champion Magazine. With

> *"These machines in the right hands can reach speeds of 35 miles per hour down the slightest gradient..."*

27

The masses of athletes and Swasie making their way towards the finish of the event

Swasie's wheelchair swept along the roads and promenade, here followed by Ally Boxie, the TV cameraman on a motorcycle

doubted him to eat their words. In the event the course offered little difficulty to Swasie apart from one long uphill stretch shortly before the finish.

The weather was fine, if anything, too fine. Swasie would have preferred an overcast day with a light shower or two. But the crowds were vocally supportive and encouraging as Swasie's wheelchair

further assistance from Volvo UK, who supplied the transport, Swasie, his son, daughter in law and camera crew arrived in Newcastle on Saturday to prepare for the following day's event. Taking advantage of his connections in the police service he was welcomed by Chief Inspector Louis Hoareau who showed him the route. Swasie and his son and daughter also had

time for a little sight-seeing in Newcastle before getting an early night in preparation for the following day's endeavours.

On the big day, Swasie was to cause all those who

Swasie dropped in on some old friends, Mia and Bill Cram, and chatted with their famous son, Steve

"Swasie would have preferred an overcast day with a light shower or two..."

"...unaware that Swasie often completed the same mileage, and sometimes far more..."

swept along the roads and promenade. Not only did he and his 'chariot' complete the 'run' in a comfortable 3 hours and 20 minutes, but on arrival at the finish he had so much strength and stamina he could easily have completed the same distance again.

All who witnessed such a 'conveyance' being propelled by arm power for such a distance were amazed. They were unaware that Swasie completed the same mileage, and sometimes far more, every single day back home on Wirral!

At the finish of the race the famous runner, Steve Cram, interviewed Swasie for Tyne Tees Television and was extremely impressed by the 'wheelchair pilot's' performance.

Coincidentally, Steve's mother Mia and father Bill (an ex-bobby) were old friends of Swasie's and they donated generously to his charity as he passed them along the route.

Swasie's beloved wife Marje, for whom he completed the run so that he could present her with his medal, hoped to be there on the day but was, sadly, too ill to attend. However, she proudly witnessed her

Swasie had some time for sight-seeing, including the famous bridge over the Tyne

husband's success as she watched the event on television back home.

On his return Swasie's first job was to proudly place the Great Northern Run medal around the neck of his beloved wife. It was *her* medal. Marje wore the medal with immense pride, fully aware of the effort her husband had made to bring the prestigious reward back.

Swasie's confidence had grown once again as yet another feat had been achieved and he sought other, equally demanding feats in his contining quest to raise money for his charity.

...he sought other, equally demanding feats in his continuing quest to raise money...

29

Swasie Turner ..... Off The Cuff

Accolades – some even for heroes!

Those serving members and their injured and retired colleagues of the 'exclusive club' – the "Emergency Services" - who are renowned for their heroic and often miraculous feats - rarely receive the true recognition they deserve.

Indeed, some feats have been so amazing that actors have repeated such incidents on screen for our entertainment, receiving astronomical salaries in the process - and at no risk!

Wirral Champion - September 1997

Swasie has always been an outspoken champion of the emergency services and in this column he highlights some of the feats of colleagues and fellow members of the exclusive club whose efforts he considered went unheralded.....

Alas, because members of the emergency services are trained to a high standard, such feats and achievements are only too often taken for granted by those whose very existence is sometimes due solely to their professional expertise and dedication. Such heroes and heroines' life saving performances, many times in the face of adversity, often go unnoticed or unrecognised.

However, if ever my trusty pen can identify and emphasise what such persons have done for the benefit of others, I will go out of my way to short circuit their usual modesty and ensure that Joe Public is made aware of who they are and what they have done. These include police officers, ambulance crews, firefighters, nurses, doctors and those selfless and courageous members of our lifeboat crews whose regular deeds of valour are usually performed out of sight of our dangerous coastline, and, as is the norm, "out of sight is out of mind!"

After many years of operational lifeboat service at Hoylake, including sixteen as coxswain, the very able and competent

> *their feats and achievements are too often taken for granted by those whose very existence is due to their professional expertise...*

30

Hoylake lifeboat is guaranteed to continue in very safe and capable hands.....

John McDermott has gracefully retired and relinquished his responsible position to the equally able and competent Dave Dodd.

Both these men are veterans of many dangerous and successful lifesaving operations out in the tempestuous seas, often in total darkness, when their own lives and those of their crew were on the line. I am proud indeed to include these two real heroes among my personal friends.

On behalf of Mr & Mrs Joe Public I would like to thank Mr McDermott, Mr Dodd and all those who have served with them for their saving of countless lives.

I remember only too well when Dave Dodd and myself recovered the body of an angler from the sea off Leasowe lighthouse. The poor man had been tragically swept out to sea from the Welsh coast a week before. Mr Dodd was the epitome of compassion and efficiency and although both of us received a soaking, he was an inspiration to those at the scene by his professionalism. I also congratulate Mr Dodd on his well deserved promotion to coxswain. Hoylake lifeboat is guaranteed to continue to be in very safe and capable hands.

In conclusion, I must include the quick thinking heroism of Mr Gordon Fair, Headmaster of Mosslands School, Wallasey. Whilst out walking on a North Wales beach with his wife, his attention was drawn to a distraught young mother whose son was completely buried in sand.

Due entirely to Mr Fair's speedy actions in finding and digging out the almost lifeless boy with his bare hands, the youngster's life was saved in the nick of time. Mr Fair has rightly been awarded a certificate for his endeavours. Congratulations and well done. I salute you.

> *...he was an inspiration to those at the scene by his professionalism...*

31

Ascent of Talacre Lighthouse

Only two days after his success in The Great North Run in Tyneside, Swasie was again in action raising precious funds for the cancer appeal.

16th September 1997

The ascent of Talacre Lighthouse, on the North Wales coast, was tackled by Swasie just two days after his Great North 'Run', but, as he had predicted, the 'run' was no 'great' problem – but this was another climb!

This time, he was granted permission by the McAlister family to climb, complete with wheelchair, their listed building, the well-known landmark, Talacre Lighthouse.

The lighthouse, at Point of Ayr, is on the North Wales coast across the Dee Estuary from Swasie's home on Wirral. Climbing Talacre would complete a trio for Swasie. He had already successfully tackled Leasowe and New Brighton Lighthouses on the Wirral peninsula.

Talacre Lighthouse, which is easily seen from the Dee coast of Wirral, was the only other surviving lighthouse in the north west area.

Swasie refused assistance to transport him over the sandhills to the lighthouse and struggled to make his own way. Accompanied by his carer, and permanent photographer, Chris Lucas, the McAlister family, numerous witnesses and the press, the party made their way over the dunes to the well-known structure.

Eventually, a sweating Swasie and his chair reached the top of the lighthouse and he made his way outside to sit on the veranda where he was photographed and interviewed by the local media. Mr McAlister jnr then presented Swasie with a very substantial cheque for his fund.

left, Swasie makes his first tentative approach to Talacre Lighthouse

> ## "He had already tackled Leasowe and New Brighton Lighthouses on the Wirral peninsula"

Although a smaller lighthouse than either Leasowe or New Brighton, Talacre had its own problems. *"Talacre was quite easy,"* said Swasie afterwards, *"It's only a tiddler really! The hardest part was actually getting to the lighthouse - the climb itself was no trouble, not after New Brighton which was a real toughie!"*

The successful event was, like those before, to receive much publicity. Swasie and his chair had now successfully climbed the three northwest coast lighthouses, New Brighton, Leasowe and, finally, Talacre.

These feats had never before been attempted or accomplished and this fact no doubt enhanced Swasie's notoriety with regard to the sheer physical efforts required to succeed with

Eventually Swasie and his chair reached the top of the lighthouse

such demanding endeavours. Swasie was now well on the way to establishing himself as a very determined fundraiser in his efforts to assist in the fight against the dreaded disease, cancer.

Unknown to our crusader at this time, this was to be the last fund raising event before the demise of Swasie's beloved Marje.

> ## "These feats had never before been attempted..."

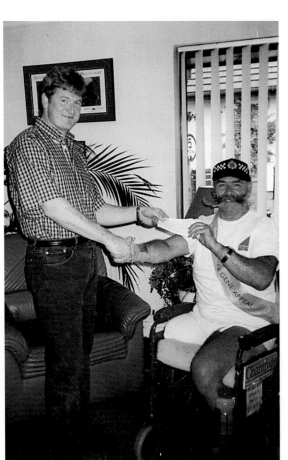

right, Swasie takes the strain as he drags his wheelchair up the steep stairs

left, James McAllister jnr. presents Swasie with a generous donation to his appeal fund

Swasie Turner .... At The Sharp End

Police assailants should be behind bars!

At Maidstone Crown Court a 15 stone man walked free after severely attacking a young female police officer, who later mis-carried.

I have utter contempt for some of our uncaring judiciary. Society demands nothing less than total protection of police officers via the courts as they courageously carry out their thankless and dangerous duties.

Has this Assistant Recorder Judge lost all his marbles? Whilst he was, no doubt, reclining in his comfortable easy chair, G & T in hand in his mansion, or sleeping safely in his four poster bed, WPC Curran, a brave young policewoman, tackled a 15 stone middle aged drunk out

Police News - February 1998

Swasie turned his attention to the treatment of people convicted of assaulting the police. He found the courts often took a totally unsympathetic line - with regard to the police, that is, not the assailants!

on our hostile streets, and was badly beaten by him with her own baton. Why on earth wasn't this inebriated drunken bully sent to jail instead of being anointed with the balm of the Judge's kindness?

It's no wonder our Police service has lost 962 officers over a five year period. There were 127,760 police officers in 1992 and these fell to 126,798 in 1997! I wonder why? Perhaps it could have something to do with morale and those lily livered judges on our benches.

The ever apprehensive Mr and Mrs Joe Public constantly live in fear of increasing crime and violence. When are the courts going to get their act

together and issue deterrent punishments which will give out a message to wrong doers loud and clear "ATTACK OUR POLICE OFFICERS AND YOU WILL GO TO PRISON."

I, too, am a 'police statistic', confined to a wheelchair after being badly and maliciously injured by an assailant whilst on duty. Due to another no doubt deprived and equally misunderstood member of society - who has never been apprehended - after causing injuries to me which caused the premature demise of my beloved career and subsequently the loss of my right leg.

No doubt, however, the taxpayers were saved considerable expense by the probable deprivation of him being sent by the courts on a 'rehabilitating' tropical holiday by the likes of Maidstone's Assistant Recorder and his benevolent colleagues on high!

> *"Whilst he reclined, G & T in hand, a brave young policewoman tackled a 15 stone drunk on our hostile streets...."*

Marjorie Turner (née Pringle)

1939-1997

After a short illness, Marje' Turner died in Arrowe Park Hospital on 12th October 1997 cradled in her husband's arms.

Marje' Pringle, as she was, was born in 1939 in Hoylake. At the age of 15 she met the dashing young man, Ron Swasie Turner from Saughall Massie, who was to be the love of her life.

They married three years later and raised two children, son Ron and daughter Jo. Swasie pursued his career and Marje worked in local bakery shops in Meols, West Kirby and Moreton, close to their home in Upton, on Wirral.

Throughout their married life Marje was the 'rock' around which the family grew. She was there when Swasie suffered horrific injuries early in his career when he was dragged along the road by a car, and again later when his face was badly smashed with a concrete block.

Since 1990 she had been a tower of strength through the traumatic aftermath of the incident which eventually ended her husband's police career.

Throughout this period Marje was always there to love, help, encourage and support Swasie.

Cruelly, after first appearing to conquer cancer, which Swasie had been raising funds to fight through the Clatterbridge Cancer Gene Appeal, it was this which was to strike Marje again, this time with tragic speed.

Swasie was at her bedside for six long days as her life slowly ebbed away and she died peacefully in his arms. In 39 years they had never been apart and they were determined that, for her last few days too, they would be together.

Christ Church, Moreton, was packed for her funeral service on Thursday 16th October 1997 with many standing outside. Moreton itself came almost to a standstill with shops closing for the duration of the service. Well over 500 people attended, testament to the popularity of this lovely lady who was known with affection by so many. She was later buried in Frankby Cemetery surrounded by hundreds of mourners.

Marjorie Turner left a heartbroken husband, Swasie, daughter Jo, son Ron and a much loved granddaughter, Taylor-Jane, on whom she doted.

The last photograph taken of Margje just weeks before her death, as she proudly wears the medal Swasie had brought back from his Great North Run.

Swasie has now dedicated his energy, his efforts and the rest of his life to the memory of his beloved Marje'. There are few who are not moved witnessing his determination to 'avenge' her death by raising funds to fight the killer disease - the disease which took the love of his life from his very arms.

Swasie and Marie pictured in 1996 during their summer holiday in

Swasie Turner ..... Off The Cuff

Yes - Nightingales in Arrowe Park!

There has been widespread, and justified, adverse publicity about the abhorrent and unpleasant scenes witnessed as one enters Arrowe Park, Wirral's largest and most modern hospital.

The sight of all the outside seats and valuable wheelchairs occupied by heavy smokers, including youngsters, visitors and dressing gown clad patients, some with life preserving drips attached, disgusts me.

Wirral Champion – November 1997
Swasie penned this column shortly after the tragic and sudden death of his sweetheart and best friend, his wife Marje, who died in Arrowe Park Hospital on Wirral in October 1997. It was a spontaneous reaction to the trauma and grief of his great loss and as such is a poignant insight to his very being.....

They give off the most unpleasant stink of offensive and life-threatening smoke to others, who, not only do NOT want it, but have to 'run the gauntlet' as they enter the building.

Newly arriving and chronically ill patients face the same life threatening fate as they go through the doors of the adjacent casualty department. What a dismal and vile scene for such a modern health establishment! The authorities continually promise that they "have the matter in hand" and are to eradicate the problem.

They intend to provide a special area for those hell bent on self destruction, but who is going to pay for it?

Perhaps some of the cash I have raised by various physical endeavours for medical research could be diverted to assist?

Yes, I am cynical, and feel justified in being so.

However - I can assure readers that there are NIGHTINGALES in Arrowe Park.

Once inside this nicotine stained hulk, on the wards, a totally different picture emerges. The nurses and

> **"Once inside this nicotine stained hulk, a totally different picture emerges on the wards..."**

staff illustrate a completely different scenario from that outside. A typical example of dedicated, professional and loving care to patients is to be seen on the ward under the control of Sister Gwen Whittington. She, I assure you, is the epitome of true professionalism to her calling - and it is seen on all of the wards at Arrowe Park Hospital. She and her team of equally dedicated nurses are true ambassadors of the nursing profession.

Not to be forgotten in my 'accolade' are the tea ladies and cleaners who also perform a very important role in the efficient running of the wards. They regularly and unhesitatingly assist the nurses with patients when asked to do so. This, of course, would not be necessary but for cutbacks by the 'establishment' ensuring the continuation of their 'fat cat' salaries, whilst underpaid nurses have to negotiate (grovel) for a living wage!

> *" I sat with my wife for six days and six nights as her life ebbed away... "*

> *" Every member of staff went to great lengths to ensure my wife received nothing but the best... "*

I know of the above scenario because I have just witnessed kindness, professionalism and dedicated care when it was administered to my beloved late wife. Every member of staff, including cleaners and tea ladies, went to great lengths to ensure my wife received nothing less than the best of everything.

I, too, was afforded their utmost care and attention during that traumatic period, as if they hadn't enough to do, what with running for bed pans, administering drugs, answering the phones, serving meals and later collecting the dirty dishes!

During that period, when I sat with my wife for six days and six nights as her life ebbed away, nothing was too much trouble for the staff. I was 'fed and watered' and eventually an enterprising nurse provided me with a camp bed (from somewhere?) to enable me to get some rest during my constant heartbreaking vigil.

I was humbled by such generosity and kindness, and this was not a one-off

situation. I witnessed others with dying loved ones in a similar situation.

Take note you 'ivory towered politicians', you haven't lived, but you will if ever this heartbreaking, but impressive treatment by such devoted people was ever to come your way! Why in hell's name don't the 'powers that be' wake up and ensure that these angels, these true 'Florence Nightingales' of Arrowe Park, and all our other hospitals, receive their true, fair and just reward to which they are entitled?

The fat cats of our establishment receive such huge salaries, financed by continuous cut backs (but not in their neck of the woods) while the 'nightingales' follow their dedicated calling. It is because such wonderful, caring servants of us all, remain and continue in that calling that they are taken for granted by assuming that they won't desert a sinking ship!

I sincerely hope that 'Nightingales' remain in Arrowe Park!

Swasie Turner .... In The Line Of Fire

'Poor cousins' of emergency services?

Although those in the fire service are true professionals, for some inexplicable reason they have always seemed the "poor cousins" of the emergency services. Firefighters do not like striking, neither do I. However, I understand when they have been forced into this position out of frustration.

Fire News – January 1998
Swasie followed his columns in Police News with another in Fire News, a sister publication - the independent national newspaper for the fire service of Britain. In typical fashion Swasie took a swipe at those whose attitudes branded the fire service as the poor cousins of the emergency services...

When reasonable requests for higher pay and standards have not been heard or have been dismissed out of hand. I remember, as I'm sure will the strikers at the time,

when I landed myself in trouble, receiving dire threats from senior officers when I used to cadge and purloin crates of beer from sympathetic licensees and

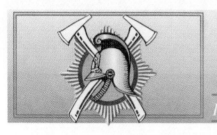
> " *I am* all for pride, formality and discipline, provided it benefits and pleases recipients and families..."

trays of fish and chips from understanding chippies, then take them, in my police Land Rover, to the lads on the brigade picket lines at Bankhall, Canning Place and other stations. Boy, did I land myself in it! But it never stopped me. I'm sure there will be firemen still serving who will remember those cadged freebies!

I intend to shout from the rooftops, the demanding role of a firefighter. I am only concerned with the well-being and welfare of those at the sharp end, those who daily risk their life and limbs on the fireground. Police officers injured and maimed on duty rightly receive publicity together with the nation's gratitude and sympathy. However, the same risks and dangers result

in just as many firefighter casualties, but these never come to the public's attention. I intend to rectify this situation which I consider mainly the fault of the powers that be. It is they who should be forceful ensuring that firefighters receive publicity and any accolades that are due.

The question of firefighters receiving medals and awards was tarnished recently when civvie

politicians on Merseyside tried to interfere with and influence the way the brigade conducted its affairs, suggesting such parades be in civilian clothing. Maybe Mr Best is not the most popular chief in the world, but I admire his stance on the matter ensuring parades continued in uniform.

Surely those attending would prefer families and friends to see such 'bull' as they receive their 'gongs'? I supported Mr Best ONLY because this stand was intended for the benefit of the lads and the tradition of the brigade and not for egotistical and vain satisfaction! I am all for pride, formality and discipline, provided it benefits and pleases recipients and families.

> "*I am* only concerned with the well-being and welfare of those at the sharp end..."

Swasie Turner ..... Off The Cuff

Morons, Coppers, Queens & Heroes

Yet again the lawless, moronic and selfish conduct of the *Pavement Cyclist* rears its despicable head. Again, a casualty has ensued and physical injury has been suffered.
TV writer Bill Ivory, standing on the footwalk outside his home, was struck by one of these 'brain dead' morons, who continually disregard and thwart our laws with apparent impunity.

Wirral Champion – December 1997
This month Swasie set about a 'breed' of minor offender that these days seems to get off Scot free, that is, if they are ever charged! He also turns his pen on some less than thoughtful senior officers who, although, 'working to the rules' are causing embarrassment for their troops.

Mr Ivory sustained a broken arm. To my knowledge, the imbecile reponsible has not been traced or prosecuted.

Perhaps, like the poor old lady struck in Wallasey in similar circumstances a short time ago breaking her hip and later dying, the perpetrator should also receive 'counselling' as was the case in Wallasey! I hope to goodness that the police take the appropriate action and prosecute in Mr Ivory's case.

The last person I reported for this offence when I was a sergeant in Wallasey, was an adult male cellarman from a local pub. He was fined £75 plus £25 costs, a nice hundred quid to remind him of his selfish and unacceptable folly.

Obviously the Magistrates on the bench at that time had more 'bottle' than there seems to be among senior police officers and prosecutors today.

Only when these 'head in the sand' pontificators see what the rest of us see, - the continual, unabated and highly dangerous conduct of a thoughtless few, will this life and limb threatening conduct be eradicated from our pavements.

> *Only when these 'head in the sand' pontificators see what the rest of us see will this life and limb threatening conduct be eradicated...*

It is with anger and sadness that I have to report that yet again some short sighted and tunnel visioned police officers among the senior ranks just cannot see the woods for the trees! They are obviously out of touch with the 'troops' at the sharp end, those front line officers who put themselves on the line for all of us.

It is difficult enough having to run the gauntlet of hostile, violent and mickey taking yobs whilst out on solo patrol in some lonely and hostile environment, or trying to pacify or control a volatile situation in a crowded licensed premises, without some of the 'Sirs' (who should know better), presenting the 'enemy' with yet more ammunition with which to 'attack' the boys and girls in blue.

South Yorkshire Police showed utter contempt for their front line bobbies by placing an advert, targeting *Homosexual* recruits, which was published in 'Gay Times' - for the *second*

> **"It is difficult enough out on solo patrol running the gauntlet of hostile, violent yobs, without presenting the 'enemy' with ammunition to 'attack' the boys and girls in blue..."**

time. This was after strong dissent was shown by members of the force the first time this was done!

They caused an outcry among the *nation's* bobbies, not just in Yorkshire. Police Federation Secretary, Paul Middup said, "*It shows the contempt that senior officers have for the vast majority of this (South Yorkshire) police force*". Officers were deeply distressed by the jibes they were receiving in pubs as a result of this advert.

The force's Deputy Chief Constable defended running the advert a second time, **against** the wishes of his men and women, those who matter out where the violence and intimidation is, **not** where he is, in the sanctuary of those ivory towers at Force HQ. He had the audacity to say, "*Publication was in line with the force's equal opportunity policy*".

Get down from your lofty pinnacle of comfortable safety and sanctuary, sir, and *listen* to your worthy, operational men and women out there taking the flak because of you and your unwanted and unappreciated 'policies'.

Perhaps you could start issuing handbags to the lads so they can hide their provocative Mace sprays, batons and handcuffs, in case they upset the 'baddies'?

Get with it sir!

> **Officers were deeply distressed by the jibes they were receiving in pubs as a result of this advert...**

United Kingdom Thugs Use Lasers....

We over the 'pond' in the UK very often hold you Americans in awe. Unfortunately, like yourselves, we in the police service are in continual conflict with our own country's persistent low life.

First the British yobs, pond life and street corner bullies, copied the American habit of wearing their baseball caps back to front as a status symbol.

American Police Beat – **January 1998**

'American Police Beat' is the national newspaper of the police forces of the USA. Swasie's reputation led to him being asked to become a regular contributor. This column, highlighting a worrying new development which started in Britain, is typical of his contributions.

Now, our ever inventive yob culture, never wanting to do an honest day's work to contribute anything of use to society, have come up with a wonderful new pastime - blinding their fellow citizens.

First of all the yobs 'arm' themselves with a laser marker pen. These are used by lecturers as pointers for their slides or overhead projection illustrations. The yobs get the pens via the usual methods, mostly thieving or shoplifting. They are certainly not getting them by legitimate purchase. To date there have been two prosecutions for this heinous behaviour;

In Leicester a perpetrator of this new phenomenon was

Shift work takes a big toll on law enforcement families. One officer speaks out on the problem. Page 4.

American Police Beat

LARGEST IN THE FIELD

Norman Spruiel is just one of 212 officers from Detroit killed in the line of duty. Story on 36 and 37.

put before the court. He was charged with assaulting a police officer by shining his laser pen into the officer's eyes and injuring him. The court stated that they wished to 'make an example' of 19 year old Mark T.......r of Oadby in hope of deterring others.

The punishment? T........r was given a 'conditional discharge'. This means if T........r behaves himself for the next 12 months he will hear no more about it and he will not have a criminal record.

I am sure that the officer involved feels completely reassured now that he knows that the judiciary will not tolerate such despicable behaviour!

> ## *Let us sincerely hope that those of the same ilk in the USA don't follow suit...*

A number of bus drivers have also been blinded since this recent craze began. Another victim rendered unemployable in his chosen calling is a train driver, blinded as he drove his packed commuter train through the suburbs of Merseyside.

A similar fate also befell a police officer. He was attempting to arrest a violent suspect when an enterprising member of the public shone a

laser pen into the officer's eyes thus facilitating the suspect's escape.

Let us sincerely hope that those of the same ilk in the USA don't follow suit. As a result of this scum and their maiming activities, decent, innocent people who genuinely require these marker pens to assist them in their work are now finding them difficult to come by because most have been banned from sale.

I wish that we over here, in the United Kingdom, were strong enough to dish out the appropriate punishment to fit the crime as you certainly seem to in the United States!

Swasie Turner is a former sergeant with the Merseyside P. D. in the UK.

> ## *I wish we over here were strong enough to dish out the appropriate punishment to fit the crime...*

Swasie Turner ..... Off The Cuff

Unhearing and Economising Mandarins

The scissor-toting mandarins of the 'Administration of Nonsensical Decisions Department' are at it again! Police, Fire Service, Hospitals, Ambulance Service - the list is endless for these faceless powers to slash at under the guise of saving pennies. Now it's the turn of the Coastguard Service.

Wirral Champion – January 1998
This month Swasie reacted to the news that the Coastguard Station at the mouth of the busy River Mersey was likely to be closed in a cost-cutting exercise. He contrasts the relatively small amount of money saved with the profligate waste going on in Europe....

How on earth can they even *think* of closing purpose-built Coastguard stations and losing professional officers? I have personal experience of these very important saviours having assisted them in a couple of rescues off Wirral's coast.

If these high flying wonders, were to be on the receiving end of such services and their own necks saved, would the services then be worthy of maintaining! I only have to mention 'Formula 1 and Tobacco' to illustrate how things 'can be arranged'!

If, after closing six Coastguard stations, even one life is lost due to such folly, that will be one life too many.

Isn't it strange how the same, penny pinchers in the corridors of power can turn blind eyes to grain barons reaping £2.1 billion compensation for price cuts which never happened, and beef and veal producers sharing £560 million because payments were 'out of line with world prices'!

> *"I only have to mention 'Formula 1 and Tobacco' to illustrate how things 'can be arranged..."*

46

The European Union's Auditors recently found 'errors' affecting £2.9 billion of taxpayers' cash. Poor book-keeping meant they could not guarantee another £12.3 billion had been spent legally!

How many Hospitals, Coastguard Stations, Fire Engines, Police Officers, Cancer Research facilities, could be financed with a fraction of that waste? I guarantee however, that no MP or MEP's pay packet has any errors! Get your European Union act together and retrieve at least some of the £5.4 billion that has been wasted. That would keep all our Coastguard stations going and buy a few fire engines as well!

To add insult to injury the Lord Chancellor, Lord Irvine, Tony Blair's highest paid minister, has spent - wait for it!! - £333,000 redecorating his official residence! An amazing £59,211 was spent on wallpaper alone! The cost of

CUT BACKS IN THE MOUNTED DEPARTMENT !!

a new fire engine! £56,066 on light fittings - that's another fire engine! We need two on Merseyside! Don't forget, tighten your belts to enable his Lordship maintain his lavish grandeur.

By the way, none of our

starved emergency services have received any cash from the National Lottery - but the 'luvvy brigade' have. They've received millions to keep their theatres afloat and for purchasing various forms of 'luvvy' paraphernalia - not fire engines! Perhaps if Glenda Jackson, the Transport Minister, had stuck to acting, in which she excelled, and abstained from interfering in the Coastguard service, things might be better. Luvvies and emergency services are not compatible!

You fat cats make cuts in your own back yard, set an example to those you are urging to tighten belts!

> "An amazing £59,211 was spent on wallpaper alone! That's the cost of a new fire engine!"

The Ascent of Blackpool Tower

After the successful completion of the 'hat trick' trio of lighthouse climbs, a chance remark in jest was to fuel Swasie's next truly eccentric endeavour!

After hearing of his lighthouse 'jaunts' a friend jokingly remarked, *"I suppose you'll be climbing Blackpool Tower next?"*

27th March 1998

The ascent of the famous Blackpool Tower was the next challenge faced by Swasie - in response to a casual comment by a friend!

Little did that person know that he had planted the seed of what would be deemed an impossibility into Swasie's mind.

The remark manifested itself in the next fundraising feat - climbing Blackpool Tower! When Swasie contacted the tower's owners, a flabbergasted Brian Crompton kindly and sympathetically listened to Swasie's request with disbelief. Eventually, however, a persistent Swasie managed to convince the astonished entrepreneur that his request was deadly serious.

top right, Swasie tackles one of the spiral staircases

left, the last vertical stage of his long climb up the exposed ladder

After a lot of convincing that the climb could be done, a very apprehensive Mr Crompton finally gave in to his better judgement and kindly gave the go ahead.

On a rainy Friday 27th March 1998, Swasie and his usual entourage (this time somewhat doubtful) met with the Tower authorities, the press and other equally sceptical persons to witness what they thought could not possibly be done.

Blackpool Tower stands a mighty 500ft high. First, Swasie had to climb concrete steps to a lift which conveyed him up to 380 feet. Then he climbed the top 120 feet via a narrow metal spiral staircase, exposed to the elements, before finally reaching two vertical iron ladders. After struggling up these he had to negotiate a trap door in the top platform to reach the tower's flagpole. Even the maintenance personnel rarely venture this high. Present during this feat were Ally Boxie, a television cameraman and Brian Crompton. Pictures were taken at the flagpole to record this amazing 'first'.

Although successful, a price was paid! Swasie broke a finger during the ascent, although he did not know at the time, having dismissed the pain as a 'hazard of his endeavours', thinking that he had just bruised his hand.

Mission completed, an extremely jubilant Swasie retraced his steps down via the same route. On reaching the ground the impressed and very kind and benevolent Brian Crompton and his staff, as well as donating a generous sum, invited Swasie to sign the very prestigious leather

right, a jubilant Swasie poses on the famous Golden Mile after the completion of his climb

below, on his way down Swasie was congratulated by Brian Crompton

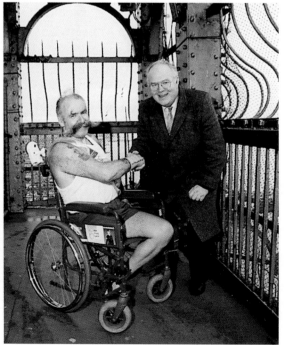

bound Visitors' Book. This 'accolade' is normally reserved for only a very privileged few, mainly VIPs.

"This really was the hardest bit of climbing I have ever done." said Swasie later, in the comfort of his home,

"..the hardest bit of climbing I have ever done...."

"The metal spiral staircase was totally open and soaking wet from the bad weather we had recently. Not only that but the wind had got up quite severely by the time I reached the last stretch and I was fortunate that the manager, Brian Crompton, allowed me to continue. The final 'leg' however, was the worst - up the vertical metal ladder to the small platform at the very top."

At the end of a tiring day, the overjoyed fundraiser returned home to consider how his next 'eccentricity' would manifest itself into an enticing fundraising event.

Swasie Turner .... At The Sharp End

Voyage rewards 'clean sheet' youths

All too often we hear about aggression and confrontation by what some would consider 'frustrated' teenagers!

We, as law abiding citizens are, rightly, all too ready to demand severe punishment of those who terrify and abuse the elderly and vulnerable - as a deterrent to others.

It is said that one of the main causes of such anti-social behaviour among teenagers, especially those from deprived or underprivileged communities, is lack of incentive or initiative, in other words, acute boredom!

When I was a Sergeant in Wallasey, I had the privilege of having a number of excellent men and women under my command including Constable Dave Ashworth. This dedicated officer has since progressed to become an enthusiastic member of the Juvenile Liaison Department. He and colleagues have now come up with a brilliant idea to encourage and reward law abiding youths to 'abide by society's rules'.

Police News – **March 1998**

Swasie's articles for the Police News covered a number of themes directly connected with the police force and his experiences drawn from his local knowledge of the force in Merseyside....

By sheer hard work they have secured the support of businesses and organisations in Wirral to help finance a 'chance in a lifetime' for underprivileged young people. For youngsters, male or female, between 16 and 24 years who live in Wirral and wish to test their ability, physically and mentally, the Liaison team have created the opportunity to go on a 'Chance of a lifetime voyage' on a sail training ship. This will develop a sense of responsibility, discipline, the ability to get on with others and to work as a team. It is not a holiday but a 12 day character and stamina builder for those who take part.

No experience is necessary but applicants, understandably, must have NO police cautions or convictions. This is right, as to deviate would send out the wrong message, which has been the case in the past.

The object is to increase the number and quality of positive police contacts with young people and local companies. This gives young adults the opportunity to meet and talk with members of the local police, at the same time building confidence and self discipline (sadly lacking in many).

I applaud Con. Ashworth and his colleagues. They have created a fantastic scheme which will be beneficial to all concerned, as well as society in general. I wish them, every success.

I hope, too, that senior officers in Merseyside Police Force acknowledge the efforts put into this initiative. Well done the Juvenile Liaison officers of Merseyside Police.

> *the main causes of anti-social behaviour among teenagers is lack of incentive or initiative, i.e, acute boredom!*

The 'Kingsway' Mersey Tunnel

14th April 1998

After pondering what next, Swasie contacted Mersey Tunnels Police for his latest adventure. A very helpful Chief Inspector John Sutherberry, already well aware of Swasie's pedigree and achievements, promised to consider whether to allow him to make a return trip to Liverpool through the tunnel - 'in a wheelchair'!

> *Swasie's constant search for 'challenges' to test himself, and to raise money for the fund by sponsorship, took him to hitherto uncharted depths - the Mersey Tunnel under the river which separates Wirral from Liverpool.*

Mr Sutherberry consulted his senior officers to see if it would be possible to allow such an unorthodox vehicle to be propelled through the tunnel to Liverpool and back in aid of charity.

This was by far the most unusual request that had ever been made to the Tunnels Police.

After lengthy, careful and extremely kind consideration, they eventually agreed, as a purely 'one-off' gesture', to allow this bizarre venture to take place. The ex-copper's latest exploit would be a real traffic stopper!

The first Mersey Tunnel, which links Birkenhead with central Liverpool, had been opened by Queen Mary in 1934 and was named Queensway in her honour. This massive undertaking, a four lane tunnel with two smaller two-lane branch tunnels, had been constructed, over a period of ten years, to alleviate the congestion on the ferry boats which at that time carried all vehicular traffic across the busy river.

However, by the late 1960s

The first Mersey Tunnel had been opened by Queen Mary on 18 July 1934

congestion in the town centre of Birkenhead and in the city of Liverpool had built up to near chaotic proportions with volumes of traffic undreamed of in the early 1930s.

Consequently, construction of a second Mersey Tunnel, subsequently to be known as Kingsway, was undertaken and this was eventually completed in 1971.

This time, though, the tunnel was actually a pair of smaller, two-lane, tunnels running alongside each other. They started in a disused railway cutting in Wallasey and linked Wirral and the M53 motorway with Liverpool.

Its opening brought relief to the, by then, congested first

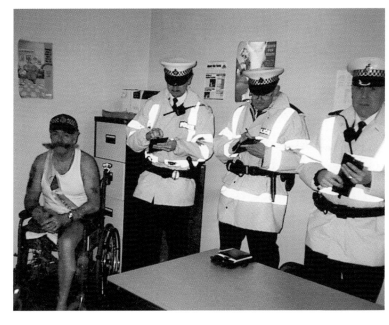

Mersey Tunnel which had been struggling to cope with the ever-increasing volumes of traffic.

And so, on Tuesday 14th

above, Swasie, after the usual quick cuppa', waits with the 'troops' to go out into the cold night air and start his return trip to Liverpool, left, through the tunnel

April 1998, a very cold 'wintery' night, Swasie arrived at the Wallasey entrance to Kingsway and paraded with the Tunnels Police night shift.

Approaching midnight, at the conclusion of the parade and after the usual quick cuppa', the 'troops' were dispersed out into the night to commence their patrols as snow started to fall. In no time the whole area lay under a thick blanket as the snow floated down relentlessly.

One of the twin tubes of the normally busy Kingsway Tunnel was closed to traffic for the night to allow essential maintenance work to be carried out.

Accompanied by a patrolling police vehicle, Swasie was photographed by the press as he posed at the pay booths before setting off on his epic trip to the big city on the other side

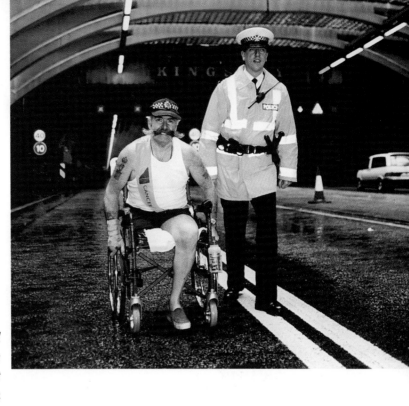

of the River Mersey nearly three miles away.

In the heavy snow, Swasie, undeterred, propelled his chair the quarter mile to the tunnel entrance and very soon resembled a mobile snowman as the large flakes floated down thick and fast. The journeys, although only a comparatively short two and a half miles each way, were nevertheless not easy.

Both the descent on entry and the subsequent climbs to the exits at the opposite ends were very long and extremely steep in gradient. There are virtually no level stretches of road inside any of the Mersey Tunnels!

Bearing in mind also that the chair had no brakes, Swasie's hands soon became raw as he continually gripped the wheels to control downward progress during the mile long descents in each direction. These were, of course, followed by the equally gruelling, long and steep climbs.

Eventually, the intrepid fundraiser reached Liverpool and made his way out in the Arctic conditions that still prevailed, once again

Swasie and his police escort emerge from the tunnel under the shelter of the entrance canopy at the end of his unique return trip

transforming him into a snowman as though he had stepped straight off the front of a Christmas card - in April!

More photographs were taken by the press and his ever present carer, Chris, to put on record the unusual feat achieved that night. After a brief respite the 57lb chair was then propelled on its equally arduous return journey back to Wirral.

Once out into the elements again at journey's end, Swasie drove his chair up a steep gradient through the thick snow and slush to the warm confines of the police office.

There, a welcome brew of tea was forthcoming and gratefully received, courtesy of Policewoman Anne Leadbetter and Inspector Neil Carney. All the officers on duty donated generously to yet again swell the coffers of the Cancer Fund on completion of the gruelling and certainly unusual feat that they had witnessed during their shift.

A jubilant Swasie then returned home to his welcoming bed, once again having completed a 'wheelchair first'!

Swasie Turner ..... Off The Cuff

Punishment for pride demeans 'the cloth'

As recognition for meritorious police service, an undercover officer was so good and successful he ought to have been rewarded by being given a 'gong'. However, instead, like others of his ilk who willingly surrender their comfortable security and family life for the benefit of the job, he has been transferred 'back to uniform duties'.

This, after moving home to live in squalor and danger among the drug pedlars, thieves and riff-raff to infiltrate the underworld. This he did with disastrous results for them!

Wirral Champion – February 1998
Swasie considers the 'punishment' of an officer being 'returned to uniform duties' and the effect such a perception has on the rank and file policemen and women. Why should it be considered a 'punishment'?

Why such ungrateful and disloyal treatment then? Well, the same officer became aware that one of his superiors was 'on a bit of a fiddle' and he didn't hesitate to make the boss aware of his contempt. The boss didn't like this and an atmosphere developed.

Just as a similar set of circumstances befell me when I was a CID officer, when I, too, was returned to 'uniformed duties'. All because I stood by a principle and 'upset the boss'.

The problem is, when this happens, there is no comeback. Trying to get back into a hard earned position is akin to urinating into the wind! An attempt to help the poor officer was made by the 'underdog's crusader', ex Merseyside ACC Alison Halford, but, alas, even her efforts have so far fallen on stoney ground.

What is really annoying, though, is the fact that to wear the uniform, 'the cloth', is deemed a punishment at all! What does this say to the backbone of the force, the lads and girls at the sharp end, out in the streets wearing their uniform with pride. To be posted into the CID is NOT a promotion, it is a TRANSFER from one department to another. Yes, being in plain clothes does have its perks, including

> *...the same officer became aware that one of his superiors was 'on a bit of a fiddle'...*

financial advancements, only because there is more overtime, plus one or two allowances. But that does not mean every officer in the force wants to be in CID, because they don't. Many are promoted to higher rank enhancing the service.

We have yet another example of 'punishing' two officers to wear 'uniform'.

Lou Matthews and Ben Houchen, late of Middlesborough's 'Zero Tolerance' squad, had the cheek(?) to take 3 suspended colleagues to the CID Christmas party. What's all this about being innocent until proved guilty? Does this mean that a Detective Chief Super who might have invited suspended Chief Ray Mallon to the same party would have been 'returned to uniform'? I somehow think not! Again one law for some, another for others.

What about officers being allowed to stay in the force in the same job with criminal convictions? Well, that's definitely not on, you might say. But what about other less criminal activities?

Recently a young Lancs Detective Constable blighted his career when he

> ## "I have attended such parties where officers let their hair down and 'high jinks' took place..."

groped a stripper and was made to pay the ultimate price - his job. This incident drew the wrath of the sirs and ma'ams, especially as the 'party' took place on police premises. Okay, the officer was naughty, as were others present. Once it came to the notice of indignant senior officers (*all of whom had never attended such a 'do' in their entire careers!*) proceedings were instituted by 'indignant' upstairs.

I cannot deny I have attended such parties where hard working officers let their hair down and 'high jinks' took place. Yes, on police premises on occasions, with senior officers in attendance as well - and they were often worse than the lads!

Imagine if a senior lady officer were 'groped' lustfully by another high ranking officer - just a 'bit of fun'? Suppose she went

home, put it down to 'canteen culture' and didn't report it. What if she were to become a top brass and was asked to deal with a similar incident involving junior officers at a party. Wouldn't it be hypocritical if a young officer were to lose his job and pension for just being naughty? But, if he had been a senior officer nothing may have come of it!

Well, such incidents, have happened, do happen and will continue to happen. The 'canteen culture' in the police service will never be extirpated, no matter how many new brooms. Boys will be boys! I agree such conduct is not becoming police officers, but let's apply the same punishment to all who let down 'the cloth'. Let us do unto others as we would be done by.

There are many skeletons in senior officer's cupboards. Some have short memories enhanced by convenient amnesia. I do not think that the Lancs officer should lose his job and career over this incident. By all means fine him, there but for the grace, as they say. I wish him well in his appeal.

> ## "...such incidents, have happened and will continue to, 'canteen culture' will never be extirpated..."

Talacre to Wirral 'Marathon'

On the lookout for challenges, Swasie decided to tackle a 'high mileage' trek in his wheelchair!

He again contacted the McAlister family at their Talacre caravan site base. This time to set off on a 41 mile journey back to Wirral and to utilise their facilities prior to departure if needed.

Swasie and his 'back up' party met at the park offices where they were given tea and refreshments as well as another generous donation! There, also, were the North Wales Police whose officers

12th May 1998

Swasie searched for 'challenges' took him in a different direction with the first of his 'endurance' marathons. This one from Talacre to his home in Wirral.

right, Mr McAlister presents Swasie with a generous donation

below, Swasie is always in touch - coming out of Flint at speed with pursuing cameraman

would keep discreet watch to ensure Swasie's safety. Though not having tackled such a distance before, Swasie was confident he could complete the journey.

On Tuesday 12th May 1998, Marje's birthday, he set out from Talacre at 10.25am, back along the beach road to the A548. The main coast road from Queensferry to Rhyl is fairly flat, running along the western shore of the Dee, and mostly dual carriageway with occasional reductions to single making the presence of the police reassuring. He went through Ffynnongroew and into the small village of Mostyn. Here the road hugs the railway, the occasional 'Sprinter' contrasting with Swasie's leisurely passage.

After passing Bagillt views of Neston and Parkgate across the Dee with its banks of reeds and marsh grass were tantalising images of 'home'. The road reduced once more to single carriageway as he made his way into Flint. This little town, sandwiched between 'Flint Mountain' and the Dee, was busy with shoppers who encouraged him on. Emerging from the town Swasie saw his first major

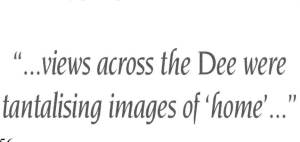

"...views across the Dee were tantalising images of 'home'..."

landmark - the majestic new Dee Bridge, recently opened to ease pressure on the existing bridges at the 'bottleneck' of Queensferry. Crossing the bridge towards Wirral, Swasie felt, though yet to reach halfway, that he was now on 'home ground'. The new roads of the estate covering the old Summers Steelworks site were again a joy to wheel on and he soon reached the A550 at Sealand.

Then came the first of the real hills up to the Shotwick turnoff. Here, where the A550 leaves the main road and turns north into Wirral, he was met by Cheshire Police who took over from their North Wales colleagues.

Then the drop into Shotwick Dip and another climb up the other side. Here too, the road was narrow and the police escort essential. After more ups and downs he reached Two Mills where the Chester High Road, linking the west coast of Wirral with Chester, runs through the beautiful countryside of South Wirral. Neston and Parkgate were passed, as he reached Gayton and the Devon Doorway where Cheshire Police handed over to Merseyside officers for the final 'leg'.

Turning off Chester High Road at Gayton, Swasie went through Barnston, the descent into the 'dale' yet another energy sapping stage. But he pressed on knowing he was now near his goal. Then it was Arrowe Park and on to Upton and the notorious Sainsbury's roundabout where traffic congestion and learner drivers are the rule. Here again his police escort ensured passage through the cars as shoppers looked on amazed as Swasie swept past. Eventually, 8¼ hours after leaving Talacre, Swasie arrived safely home in Upton. He had completed non-stop a total distance of 41 miles.

Due to wide media coverage of this mammoth trek, and a live radio interview en-route, farmers had alighted from

above, Swasie makes his way over the majestic new Dee Bridge, below left, 'SLOW' was the word as he climbed up out of Barnstondale as he neared journey's end

tractors, motorists stopped their cars, lorry drivers got down from their cabs, all donating generously into the little plastic bucket on the handles of Swasie's chair. Shoppers, pub patrons and children also contributed, in total he raised over £300. The lengthy road journey had not only involved crossing the new Dee Road Bridge, but also tackling many stamina sapping, long, steep hills.

Sore and skinless hands couldn't diminish the elation of this latest success. Although the distance had again 'broken new ground' Swasie was already casting his sights at further, longer, record breaking distances.

Swasie Turner .... In The Line Of Fire

True professionalism and vulnerability!

Just in case penny-pinching mandarins of Whitehall read this column I'll draw attention to what goes on outside their privileged world.

Fire News March/April 1998

Swasie enjoyed himself this month with a couple of accolades but also a series of 'sideswipes' at all manner of stupidity, waste and just plain nonsense in the fire service which he once graced.

They enjoy freebie lunches and banquets, cocktail parties, holidays abroad with wives or mistresses, wallpaper at £300 per roll - all courtesy the frustrated taxpayer.

Recently, while this was going on a one year old baby girl in Bradford stopped breathing. Her terrified, but quick thinking, father carried her into a nearby fire station and sought assistance. (He clearly appreciated just how highly trained and professional firefighters are.)

Whilst an ambulance was summoned, firefighters, using resuscitation equipment, revived the child. They restored her pulse and breathing and, thankfully, baby Kennedy later recovered in hospital. The overjoyed and grateful parents just couldn't thank the fire brigade enough.

Although this was a fantastic result, we know this is par for the course of firefighting work. However, this does not diminish the skill and professionalism involved in saving a life, it highlights just how good brigade personnel are.

Talking about fat cats (those who don't have to beg a decent living wage risking life and limb, and don't have to threaten strike action to achieve basic rights) how's this for extravagance?

The European Parliament installed 158 showers for Euro MPs (who do a dirty, demanding, dangerous day's work!) at a cost of £7,000 .... EACH! An indignant spokesman answered criticism saying "I don't think £7,000 is a lot compared to the normal cost of showers!" He obviously didn't mean fire station showers!

Now, off on another tangent - Members of our numerous brigades will no doubt be pleased to know that Staffordshire Police have become the first force in the UK to have direct links with the fire service with a new £6m communications system.

The overjoyed and grateful parents just couldn't thank the fire brigade enough...

The new Starnet system will allow 'operational' police officers at incidents and fire officers to be put into 'talk groups' (the phraseology department are at it again!) so that they can talk to each other directly.

The National Public Safety Radio Communications Project aims to connect all branches of the emergency services 'eventually' but not until 2003. Mmm! Five more years eh? Why on earth the emergency services - Police, Fire, Ambulance, Coastguard and RNLI have not been totally connected before is a mystery.

'Verbal' liaison between those same services existed in this country during the Second World War, so how come it's taken so long to get things moving now?

I do, however, say "Well done Staffordshire" but this should have been done years ago!

Now, on another note, I remember only too well in the not too distant past, how

...a firefighter was injured on duty while he fought a fire deliberately started by some local yobs...

some fire chiefs were worried about firefighters being 'overweight' or 'out of condition'. They were thinking of introducing a regular dose of PT to combat this - but not for those in office or day jobs! Well, Avon firefighters keep themselves fit between shouts playing volleyball. However, the 'sirs' in the Avon Brigade have decided to stop this because it 'leads to too many injuries'.

So, you firefighters who enjoy your weekend games of football, cricket or tennis etc, had better watch out!

In conclusion, I wish to draw attention to those who should be doing more to

protect our firefighters at the fireground. Be it the police, the judiciary or those political mandarins, you all have an obligation to ensure the safety of our fire crews.

There wouldn't half be some comments from the do-gooders if the lads turned an inch and a half branch at 60lb pressure on the yobs who attack them as they put out fires, while they stand, baseball caps on back to front, gawping and verbally abusing our heroes.

Recently, yet again, a firefighter was injured on duty, totally unneccesarily while he fought a fire which had been deliberately started by some local yobs. Casualties in the brigade are mounting alarmingly due to the scum of our society who carry out these arson attacks. Those responsible should be hunted down mercilessly, then ruthlessly punished by lengthy terms of incarceration, better still throw away the key!

I reiterate, the best place for such scum is at the end of a jet from a main branch before they are put away!

...liaison between those services existed during the Second World War, so how come it's taken so long to get things moving?

The Circuit of Anglesey's Coast

The consistent daily roadwork of ten to twenty plus miles continued as Swasie set out in the early hours each morning. Such distances were now no effort as he sought new goals of endurance and greater distances to complete.

Tuesday 23rd June 1998 was to see Swasie's greatest feat of endurance to date, a clockwise 'circumnavigation' of the coastal roads of Anglesey.

23rd June 1998

Swasie's second 'marathon challenge' took him to the beautiful Isle of Anglesey just off the North Wales coast where he and Marje and the family had spent so many happy holidays.

Setting off from the Britannia Bridge, which takes both rail and road traffic across the Menai Straits onto Anglesey, Swasie commenced this challenge, accompanied by his back up team and a single police car.

above, Swasie commenced this challenge from the slip road of the famous Britannia Bridge

below, which takes both rail and road traffic across the Menai Straits onto Anglesey

Over the years Swasie and Marje had enjoyed numerous holidays with their children on the beautiful Welsh island of 'Ynys Mon', the Welsh name for Anglesey. This popular island is renowned for its beauty and is a favourite venue for tourists and holidaymakers every year, particularly during the warm summer months.

Although quite a large island, Swasie had decided to attempt a wheelchair 'circuit' and, after contacting the usual authorities, arrangements were made for this to be his next venture.

Press, radio and TV

announced the event. Consequently, at 8.40am on a very wet and windy autumn morning, Constable Peter Powell, the local bobby from Menai Bridge, ensured that an already very wet Swasie set off safely from the Britannia Bridge on this giant trip.

Constable Powell and his colleagues did not believe that the distance would be completed, first due to the mileage involved but also due to the hilly terrain on parts of the island which would have to be negotiated.

It was a lonely journey for much of the route. The early morning and the late

right, the well known property of Plas Newydd overlooks the Straits

below, the most famous railway station sign in Britain

evening saw little traffic or crowds and along stretches of open country, particularly on the north coast, the unremittingly isolation was numbing. However, during the heat of the day hundreds

turned out in the small towns and villages to watch the amazing sight of Swasie and his handlebar moustache powering along the road in his standard DHS wheelchair.

The first few miles were along the old A5 from the Britannia Bridge towards the almost unpronounceable Llanfairpwllgwyngyllgoger-chwyrndrobwllllantysiliog-ogogoch, now avoided by most of the traffic which uses the new by-pass. Just before reaching LlanfairPG, under the shadow of the Marquess of Anglesey's column, Swasie turned off onto the A4080 which makes its way leisurely along the Menai Straits coast past the famous National Trust property of Plas Newydd, the home of the Marquess.

The road is gentle and sheltered as it meanders through the lush woodland and rolling fields of this part of the island.

Police officers utilised their normal patrols to keep an

LLANFAIRPWLLGWYNGYLLGOGERYCHWYRNDROBWLLLLANTYSILIOGOGOGOCH

> ## "the amazing sight of Swasie and his handlebar moustache powering along the road in his standard DHS wheelchair...."

left, as the road meanders through the countryside the views across the Straits towards Snowdonia were superb

61

Ynys Mon - The Isle of Anglesey -
Swasie's route of 'circumnavigation'

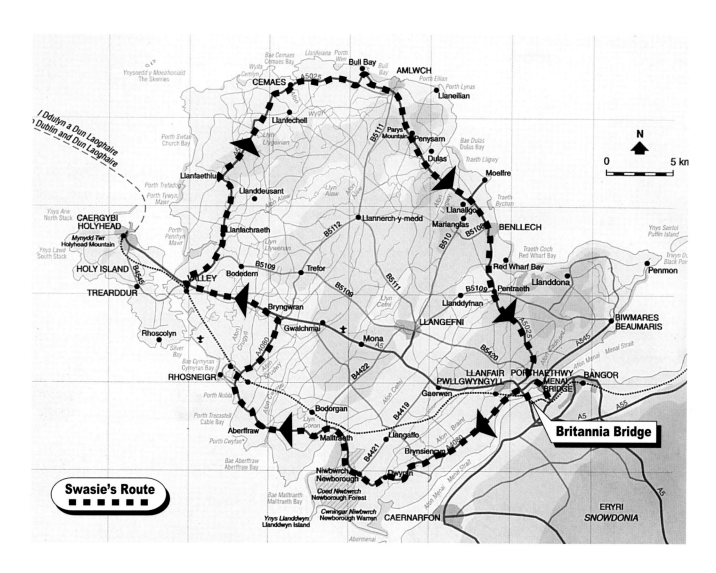

Whilst Anglesey is basically a diamond in shape, the west
and east corners are relatively cut off from the main body
of the island.

The separate western island of Holyhed is linked by two
bridges to the 'mainland' and is the busy port linking with
Ireland. The eastern corner, including Beamaris and
Puffin Island, although it is a very popular part of the
island with visitors and holidaymakers is similarly off the
beaten track,.

Swasie chose to stay on the 'mainland' principally
following the A4080 and A5025, with a short stretch of the
busy A5 flung in for good measure!

eye on the wheelchair pilot as he slowly, but surely, consumed mile after mile of the island's roads. For the first few hours the rain was persistent and heavy, although this did not worry a very determined vest and shorts clad fundraiser, as his powerful arms propelled him along. Would his strength and stamina prevail, however, for such a long distance?

Swasie swept through the small village of Brynsiencyn and went on to Dwyran. The scenery was now gradually changing to a sea coast - less trees, and these were leaning over, blown by the prevailing winds off the Irish Sea. However, the going was easy and level as he approached Newborough, where a large Forestry Commission plantation has become a nature reserve and a popular holiday spot with its superb beach at Llandwyn. After the shelter of the forest section it was out again across the open sandy approaches to the fishing village of Malltraeth sitting peacefully on a gentle inlet.

right, he moved on towards Aberffraw where the silhouette of St Gwyfan's Church seemingly rises from the sea

Again motorists and residents gave generously as he passed them. He was continually fed and watered 'on the hoof' by his protective carer, Christine Lucas, who also photographed the epic journey as the miles rolled by. The road began to climb now as he moved on to Aberffraw where the silhouette of St Gwyfan's Church seemingly rose from the sea. Then it was on to Rhosneigr, the main holiday resort on the west coast. Here rolling seas come in

across miles of golden sands making it a mecca for watersports enthusiasts.

At this point Swasie had to turn back inland as there is no suitable road across the flat western corner of the island which includes the airfield at RAF Valley. Here the constant roar of jet engines heralds the movements of training aircraft based at this establishment as they land and take off again in continual repetition. RAF Valley is famous for many helicopter rescue missions flown from this base.

Back onto the A5, but this time a very busy A5, full of traffic rushing to and from Holyhead and its connecting ferries to Ireland. Here the road was single carriageway and Swasie needed all the protection of the police car to ensure his safety, but at

> **For the first few hours the rain was persistent and heavy, although this did not worry a very determined fundraiser...**

> **...the road was single carriageway and Swasie needed all the protection of the accompanying police car...**

least the weather was improving.

The road climbed and fell as it switchbacked for several miles to Valley itself, a small town huddled around a cross-roads, the gateway to Holyhead Island, the port and of course, to Ireland.

Holyhead Port sits at the foot of its mountain and is the commercial and industrial centre of Anglesey. Ferries sail daily to Dun Laoghaire and Dublin linking with the trains in the harbourside station. Throughout the 19th century this rail and sea link was the main route from

London to Dublin for goods and passengers, but today the bulk of the traffic comes by road. Just outside the town the chimney of the massive Aluminium works, which provides employment for many local people, is a landmark seen for miles.

Holyhead Island also includes the holiday destinations of Treaddur Bay and Rhoscolyn with their sandy beaches and boating facilities and the magnificent lighthouse on the rocky promontory of South Stack.

But there was no time to take in any of these, here, at

above, Rhosneigr, the main holiday resort on the west coast where rolling seas come in across miles of golden sands

left, the magnificent lighthouse of South Stack, not yet climbed by Swasie, stands on a rocky promontory

Valley, Swasie turned north onto the A5025 and away from the frenetic traffic of the A5. Keeping as close as physically possible to the coastline he wheeled his way through small towns and villages in what turned out to be his most ambitious and punishing 'ride' to date.

Through Llanfachraeth and Llanfaethlu he laboured northward. The west coast is littered with small bays and golden beaches most of which are approached by steep narrow lanes. Swasie kept to the main road and pressed on relentlessly towards Cemaes and the dark looming mass of Wylfa Nuclear Power Station. This great monolith stands on the headland just outside Cemaes Bay, a symbol of modern technology on an island that often appears as though time has passed it by.

Wylfa – a symbol of modern technology on an island that somehow time has passed by...

left, Swasie and his pal, 'Skippy' Jackson in Bull Bay in the summer of 1966

right, Point Lynas where Liverpool pilots board the incoming ships

> *...the north coast with its open countryside offered little shelter...*

Swasie had no time to enjoy the pleasures of the small bay and harbour for which Cemaes is famed as he struggled on towards Bull Bay and Amlwch. He was travelling along the north coast now, with its bare open countryside offering little shelter as the wind blew across the landscape.

After almost fifty miles, Swasie's, by then, skinless hands had to be cleaned and dressed. (His hands were also his brakes!) They were attended to by the kind proprietors of the Bull Bay

Hotel, Mr & Mrs Sinar. Minutes later, hands repaired, he continued his trek.

From Bull Bay, with its famous golf course and spectacular small cove, he pressed on into Amlwch and Point Lynas where the Liverpool pilots board the incoming ships. Then he turned south towards Parys Mountain. Now came the hills! Parys Mountain itself has long been a mining area where rich copper deposits

employed hundreds of local people in the busy days of the turn of the century.

The hillside itself is pock-marked with pits and shafts and pools of copper coloured water of unknown depths - a playground offering danger around every corner for the unwary!

Swasie pressed on over the hills to Penysarn. Some were long and steep and, as the miles rolled by under his wheels and castors, daylight was now fading fast. After Penysarn the road dropped steeply to the inlet at Dulas where a large landlocked tidal pool is fed by a small river from the hills. Then it was up the other side and on towards Llanallgo and Moelfre.

Although his chair was well

left, Swasie painted the holiday cottage in Amlwch that the family had stayed in during their holiday in 1964

its shingle beach and its clustered white painted cottages, is a popular holiday centre and is just a mile or so north of the famous beach and bay at Traeth Bychan.

It was there in 1939 that the tragic submarine Thetis, which went down with 99 casualties during its trials in the Irish Sea, was eventually beached.

left, Moelfre, which is perhaps, one of the most scenic bays in the whole island

right, Swasie pauses for breath on one of the many steep hills on this side of the island

But Swasie had no time for site-seeing and, anyway, its was now very dark and very wet again. The last 15 miles were covered slowly in

illuminated fore and aft, Swasie was also highlighted by the headlights of Chris's 'back up' car as well as the regular presence of the police, their blue strobe lights piercing the otherwise black night. Swasie didn't drop into Moelfre, which is perhaps, one of the most scenic bays in the whole island. This rocky cove with

left, the beautiful little village of Red Wharf Bay was passed in the darkness

" It was at Traeth Bychan in 1939 *that the Thetis, which went down with* 99 *casualties, was beached...*"

> ## *the last 15 miles were covered slowly in almost total darkness...*

almost total darkness. Benllech, another popular holiday resort, and the beautiful Red Wharf Bay were but twinkling lights as the small convoy plodded onward.

Eventually, after another steep and numbing climb out of Pentraeth, at long last, the little entourage dropped down the hill into Menai Bridge. The elegant, famous Menai Bridge itself was finally and painfully reached at 2.50am the following morning.

A full circuit of the island from Britannia Bridge to Menai Bridge had been successfully completed, the massive 72 miles virtually non-stop in an equally massive 18 hours!

At the finish the rain poured down incessantly, but a jubilant Swasie was unaware of the saturating icy droplets, to him it was

above, the elegant and famous Menai Bridge itself was finally (and painfully) reached the following morning

left, Swasie pressed on and the miles rolled by under his wheels and castors, here stopping to receive a donation from a motorist

as refreshing as nectar.

The kind and benevolent people of Anglesey had illustrated how impressed they were by their generous donations throughout the whole of the trip, even during the hours of darkness of the latter miles.

At one point way out in the country, a frail old lady came out of her little cottage and thrust a plastic bag containing thirty pounds in fifty pence pieces into Swasie's grateful, sore hands. No doubt this was a large chunk of the old lady's savings.

At another point a motorist stopped and donated a twenty pound note. These sacrificial efforts increased Swasie's enthusiasm to continue with and finally to complete 'the impossible'.

Swasie Turner ..... Off The Cuff

Michael Winner's a real winner

Patriotism in the UK is nothing compared to that shown by Americans to their emergency service heroes.
Recently the US capital hosted contingents of the nation's police forces as they paraded with pride to honour fallen comrades.

Wirral Champion – August 1998
This month Swasie had seen the way in which the American police were honoured by their state and their citizens and he compared the way in which we here in Great Britain treat our 'heroes'.....

Officers, from every part of the United States, later gathered at the National Law Enforcement Memorial near the capital, an honour we have yet to bestow on our fallen police and firefighters.

The Vice President of the United States, Mr Al Gore, personally attended and delivered a keynote speech. The service, like a candle-lit vigil held earlier, also heard speeches and accolades

YOU'RE NEW AREN'T YOU ?

Swasie

from other VIPs, together with music and prayers. Rows of 'survivors', family, friends and colleagues of those officers 'left behind' were seated before the elevated stage as guests of honour. Flanking the stage were hundreds of officers and members of the public who stood to pay their respectful homage.

Here in **Great** Britain, however, the police service have at least one fiercely loyal and appreciative supporter and benefactor, Mr Michael Winner, the film mogul, who, fortunately, has friends 'in high places'.

Like so many of us, Mr Winner was deeply moved by the murder of WPC Yvonne Fletcher, the young policewoman shot dead in London in 1984. If that murder had taken place in the US there's no way the perpetrators would have been allowed to fly back home under the guise of 'diplomatic immunity'. But then again, we're British

All who have died in the service of their country should NEVER be forgotten

memorials should be erected honouring such heroes who paid the ultimate price in service...

aren't we?

After this incident, a furious Mr Winner suggested memorials should be erected honouring such heroes who paid the ultimate price in service. He approached the Charities Commission asking for such a charity to be formed. He put his money where his mouth is and offered £5,000 to get the operation 'off the ground'.

However, would you believe it? A charity commissioner informed Mr Winner insensitively, "You intend to put up memorials to - *'mere policemen'*?". The arrogance of the man! "Yes", snapped Mr Winner, "that's exactly what I'd like to do". The commissioner replied, "We'd never allow that. That's not a charity, it's out of the question". The bowler hatted wonder quickly received a broadside from an irate Mr Winner and was rebuked. In no time Mr Winner's 'persuasive insistence' brought about a change of mind and the charity was formed.

We now have 22 such memorials throughout the UK honouring 26 police officers. That's a wonderful start. Let's hope we can

now go on like the Americans and have a national memorial to our heroes and political recognition. They deserve nothing less.

How I wish there were more people like Mr Michael Winner, especially in the corridors of power. The nation would benefit if government ministers were of his calibre and integrity, a man of courage and far sightedness. Such benevolent, intelligent gutsy men and women are sadly lacking in our corridors of power and that is why we in the UK do not match those in the US as they look after the benefits, welfare and interests of their emergency services.

I advocate posthumous accolades to ALL members of the emergency services who pay the ultimate price. All have died in the service of their country and should NEVER be forgotten. Take note complacent mandarins it's high time you changed your attitude and listened to those who know and care and, in the case of MPs, those who elected you! .... I take my hat off to, and personally thank, Mr Michael Winner.

Circuit of Chester's City Walls

Swasie approached the Cheshire Constabulary, whose Chief Constable, Mr Nigel Burgess, kindly offered assistance in an attempt on a circuit of the Roman walls of Chester.

To ensure all went well, 'Mo' Parker of Chester Tourist Office, attended at the start, where she not only presented Swasie with a model Roman Centurion, but also provided an escort in the form of a 'real' Centurion in full regalia.

13th August 1998

Our 'centurion' was Paul Harston, who had cut short his holiday in Anglesey to attend as Swasie's escort. Two police officers also accompanied the Centurion and our intrepid trekker and on the day Swasie was seen off by members of Cheshire Fire Brigade who added colour to the scene by turning out two fire engines.

Swasie commenced his circuit of the walls opposite the Police Headquarters overlooking the famous Roodee Racecourse, where

Chief Constable, Nigel Burgess wishes Swasie luck as he sets off on his circuit of the walls

flat-race meetings, the first in 1539, are held each year from May to September. It is, reputedly, the oldest racecourse in the country.

The name Roodee comes from the old English words 'rood' or cross and 'eye' or island - meaning literally the 'island of the cross. In the middle of the course is the stump of a medieval cross.

However, long before the Roodee racecourse was established on this silted

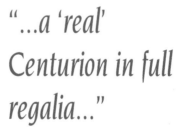

"...a 'real' Centurion in full regalia..."

left, the famous Roodee Racecourse

right, the send off team with their 'Centurion'

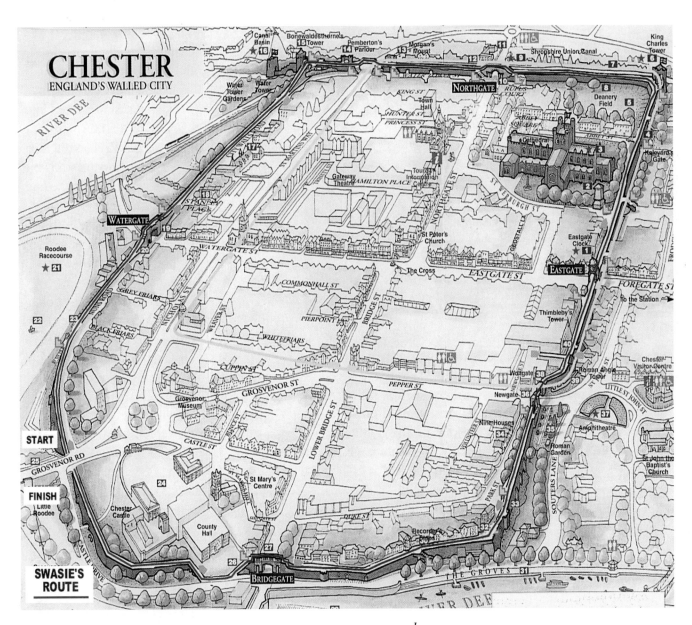

CHESTER
ENGLAND'S WALLED CITY

above, Swasie's route took him on a complete circuit of Chester's famous city walls dating from Roman times.

land alongside the river, the waters had once lapped up against the city walls at the Roman Quay where ships unloaded luxuries from the Mediterranean for their legionary garrison in this Roman outpost.

Continuing along the walls, Swasie passed behind the course's County Stand alongside Nun's Road and approached the famous Watergate. Here he met the first real obstacle, the steps up and over this famous old entrance to the city.

Watergate once gave access to the wharves of the port of Chester which, from Norman times until well into the eighteenth century had been one of the busiest ports in the north west of England. The present Watergate is relatively 'modern' having been rebuilt in 1789!

Having successfully negotiated the first obstacle Swasie continued northward along the well kept walls with fine views across to the modern industrial and commercial area of Deeside and Sealand.

The weather was fine and the small entourage of 'Centurion', policeman,

policewoman, Swasie and Chris, his carer, were joined by a group of curious visitors who were amazed at Swasie's courage and enthusiasm.

The next notable landmark was the northwest corner where Bonewaldesthorne's Tower stands. This was also once lapped by the waters of the Dee, but in the Middle Ages the river changed course due to silting and the newer Water Tower was constructed to protect the quays of the port. This was connected by a short spur wall, to the main city walls. During the Civil War of 1643-46 the Water Tower was severely pounded by cannon fire, but remains today the most complete of the original towers.

Swasie was now moving eastwards along the northern section of the walls towards Pemberton's Parlour, all that remains of what was once a huge round tower. Then it was over the relatively new bridge spanning the ring road. This is one of the few modern parts of the walls, the smooth paving offering a welcome relief from the often uneven stone slabs of the older sections, although the steps proved a small problem to progress.

Sections of the wall are accessible for 'normal' wheelchair users by ramps, and the paving is smooth and level making progress easy, however, the north wall has no such access, but this was not a problem for Swasie.

left, the Water Tower was pounded by cannon fire during the Civil War of 1643-46, but is the most complete of the original towers

below, Swasie was joined by a small group of curious visitors who were amazed at Swasie's courage and enthusiasm

The wall now started climbing gently up towards the Northgate, running alongside the deep chasm housing the Shropshire Union Canal. This had formerly been the old Roman ditch or fosse protecting the walls but had been enlarged in the late eighteenth century by canal builders to form the course of their new canal. It was steady climbing along this section eventually reaching Northgate, the highest point on the walls. Again steps proved to be but a small obstacle to the amazement of watching followers. From Northgate the views were magnificent - as far as the Welsh hills in the hazy distance.

The present gate is of Georgian design dating

"...the smooth modern paving offered a welcome relief..."

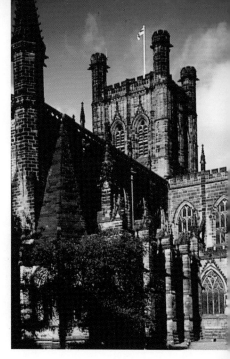

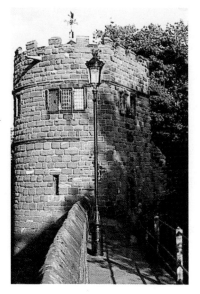

left, King Charles Tower was almost completely rebuilt in 1658

damaged during the Civil War, that it was almost completely rebuilt in 1658. The going now was fairly easy, past Kaleyard's Gate, which used to open onto the monks' kitchen gardens, past the east Window of Chester Cathedral. The cathedral itself, although dating from the 7th century had been largely restored in Victorian times and its external appearance belies its true age and history.

Swasie was now approaching one of the most dramatic parts of the tour, the Eastgate and its famous clock. Here the wall rises up between the tight knit

buildings and emerges over Eastgate Street with views into the city towards The Cross and out of the city along Foregate Street. This is very much the commercial heart of the city and the walls here were thronged with both visitors and local shoppers. As he had done all along the walls so far, Swasie paused to be

from early nineteenth century replacing the fortified mediaeval gateway which had doubled as the city's gaol. Originally, of course, this had been the site of the Roman entrance, the Porto Decumana.

The walls now levelled out as the small convoy and its enthralled 'followers' moved on towards the northeast corner and King Charles Tower. Inside the city walls the scenery now changed to the pleasant open space of Deanery Field where, in Roman times, the barrack blocks for the legionaires once stood.

King Charles Tower, at the corner where the walls turn southwards, was so badly

right, Swasie paused to be photo- graphed with tourists both on the steps and under the clock

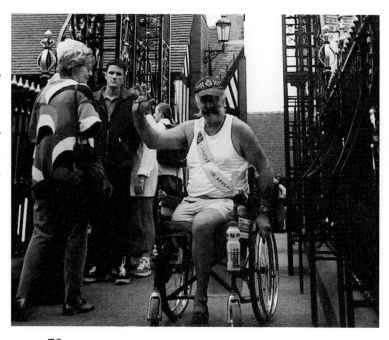

left, Eastgate Clock is at the busy commercial heart of the city thronged with both visitors and local shoppers

above, at Newgate a short set of steps proved only a temporary obstacle to Swasie as he powered on towards the river...

photographed with tourists both on the steps and under the clock. His accompanying 'Centurion', the police presence and the 'Wheelchair Pilot' himself offering a unique 'photo opportunity' for many surprised visitors.

After a brief pause for the view and photos, Swasie pressed on southwards and downwards towards the river once more. Again the going, though often narrow and uneven, was fairly easy as they made their way past

the Grosvenor Hotel and the backs of much of the commercial heart of Chester.

Then it was out past the foundations of the old Roman Angle Tower into the open aspect over the Roman Amphitheatre which could be seen just below the walls. The next landmark was Newgate spanning Pepper Street. Again a short set of steps proved only a temporary obstacle to Swasie as he powered on towards the river.

The wall was falling steeply now as he approached the Watch Tower, deeply pitted with the cannon fire of the Civic War siege, and he went down the famous Wishing Steps. Then the wall turned once more as it reached the river. Swasie was now on the 'final leg' westward back to the starting point. The river was alive with small boats and pleasure craft and the banks were thronged with tourists feeding the ducks and swans. Here the river forms a large lake behind the Chester Weir which was built in 1087 to provide water power for the old mill on the opposite bank. As a result a wide stretch of navigable water winds back

left, the river was alive with small boats and pleasure craft and the banks were thronged with tourists

"medieval Bridgegate was heavily fortified with twin towers..."

upstream providing a superb setting for boat trips or just rowing around.

Proceeding along this southern section Swasie approached Bridgegate, or Welshgate, where Lower Bridge Street emerges from the city and crosses the famous Old Dee Bridge. The medieval Bridgegate was heavily fortified with twin towers but this was largely destroyed in 1645 by cannon fire, the present gate being rebuilt in 1782.

Until 1832 the Old Dee Bridge was the only crossing of the Dee into Wales and as such was a strategically important point. The present seven arched stone bridge was

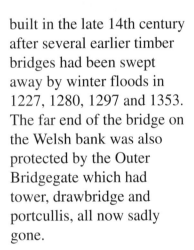

right, streetlights reflect in the waters of the river in this view of the Old Dee Bridge

built in the late 14th century after several earlier timber bridges had been swept away by winter floods in 1227, 1280, 1297 and 1353. The far end of the bridge on the Welsh bank was also protected by the Outer Bridgegate which had tower, drawbridge and portcullis, all now sadly gone.

Bridgegate again had steps to negotiate both up and down but from now on the going was relatively easy as Swasie passed the site of the old Shipgate or Sheepgate which used to give access to a ford across the river just below the Old Dee Bridge. Then it was up a gentle ramp as Chester Castle came into view. This

grandiose Greek style building, constructed in the 18th century replaced the old castle. The original, with its round towers and encircling walls, once guarded the port and the strategic river crossing.

The last few hundred yards of gentle smooth paving brought Swasie finally back to Grosvenor Road and the dominating building of the Police Headquarters, which now 'guard' this entrance to Chester. Swasie thanked his escorts, both 'Roman' and police and, particularly, the small band of enthusiastic followers who had accompanied him on this delightfully scenic, though at times, strenuous circuit of the city walls of Chester.

left, The Cross stands at the very heart of this ancient city, where the four main streets, Eastgate, Northgate, Watergate and Bridge Street meet

...this delightfully scenic circuit of the old city walls of Chester...

Swasie Turner ..... Off The Cuff

Obscene Recompense Generates Venom

I have *always* been supportive of anyone wronged in *any* way, either within or out of, *'the cloth'*. Indeed I took some flak from colleagues (of all ranks) who didn't know better when I staunchly stood by a 'very wronged' colleague, Alison Halford during her time of acute crisis when she took on the 'Establishment'. However, I am, like so many, absolutely 'brassed off' at the bleating of *some* female police officers who cry 'sexual harassment' whenever things don't go to plan.

Wirral Champion – September 1998

Swasie returns this month to a pet theme - compensation payments - and highlights some absurd sums (in his opinion) paid out to female officers, in particular, who have supposedly suffered 'sexual harrassment'.

Having spent a quarter of a century at the sharp end, I *do* admit to having witnessed *many* incidents of the so called 'canteen culture' where officers have verbally abused colleagues of the opposite sex and which has, yes, included the occasional 'touching up' - in *both* directions!

This conduct, I agree, is not acceptable, but, in most cases officers, *especially policewomen,* have dealt with offensive colleagues *quite adequately* themselves. I have found that policewomen have always more than 'held their own' and put objectionable male colleagues in their place.

When things go too far, yes, I *do* agree to an official complaint being made if this is the only solution. If matters warrant it, by all means those who perpetrated sexual harassment or bullying of colleagues should be dealt with accordingly.

What then causes my fury? I hear you ask.

Well, I have so far managed to contain myself when I

> *Having spent a quarter of a century at the sharp end, I admit to having witnessed incidents of the so called 'canteen culture'...*

read and hear of ridiculous sums of money being awarded for so called 'harassment' or slander. In severe cases I agree that the victim should be adequately compensated, but - cases where someone has not been allowed into this or that department, or they consider their career has been 'obstructed', does **not** in my opinion warrant the huge sums of money that have been awarded.

A recent *'huge'* sum of money awarded to a WPC was, in my opinion, quite rightly referred to by a national newspaper as an "Obscene Joke!"

The newspaper stated that: *"No one should have to put up with abuse at work, Sexual, Racial or Religious harassment is quite properly against the law. It is only fair that anyone who has suffered should get compensation - but £300,000 for being the butt*

> ## someone who considers their career has been 'obstructed', does **<u>not</u>** in my opinion warrant the huge sums of money awarded....

of obscene taunts is totally outrageous, especially when it is tax payers' money. This female Detective Constable has certainly hit the jackpot. She's retired on a pension (at 42) and has won a massive payout. She's also receiving counselling for stress!"

I am in **total** agreement with the newspaper as it went on to say, *"The whole compensation 'culture' has become an obscene joke. Look at the paltry sum of*

£18,000 offered to young Josie Russell for the shock of seeing her mother murdered" (and the equally paltry sum for my permanent loss of limb and disability!)

The paper quite justifiably asked, *"Are we really expected to believe that a WPC with 14 years experience as a copper was such a shrinking violet that she couldn't handle a few foul mouthed colleagues? Where had she been on patrol - Toytown?"*

My *own* WPC colleagues were *definitely* made of sterner stuff, that's for sure. It's no wonder there's dissent among older members of the service who have long memories. One wonders what the job's coming to? I must admit, such astronomic awards literally make me feel sick and extremely angry.

I am now going to place my pen into a jar of cold water to cool down!

> ## Are we to believe that a WPC with 14 years experience was such a shrinking violet she couldn't handle a few foul mouthed colleagues?

Swasie Turner .... At The Sharp End

I was invited to the 'Heartbeat' TV set in Goathland by my old friend Derek Fowlds and I stayed with the cast at the Mallyan Spout Hotel - strongly recommended!

Derek, as you will know, has starred in many popular TV and theatre shows, ranging from Basil Brush to 'Yes Minister' and many others. He is now ex-sergeant Oscar Blaketon, the Aidensfield postmaster.

I always maintain that 'nice people are at a premium' and I include Derek and his 'Heartbeat' colleagues in that category. On arrival I was given a warm welcome by

"Derek's portrayal of Blaketon, above, was the grumpy disciplinarian we all knew"

Kazia Pelka, Bill Simons, Bill Maynard and Jason Durr.

Needless to say the whole cast and staff of 'Heartbeat' are extremely pro-police and are keen to be 'updated' as to the exploits of our men and women of 'the cloth'.

Of all police series on national television, I consider Yorkshire TV's Heartbeat to be the most

accurate. 'The Bill' also portrays a realistic scenario, but 'Heartbeat' portrays authentically life in the 'job' during the sixties.

I well remember an old pal of mine, a constable in the then Cumberland, Westmoreland & Carlisle force, when we were young recruits at Bruche in 1965. He was a real 'Heartbeat' bobby out in the 'sticks' of the Yorkshire Moors. I last heard from him a couple of years ago when he was a uniformed sergeant at Carlisle. He will have retired by now - but I bet he was a right old 'Sergeant Blaketon!

Derek Fowlds' portrayal of Blaketon was the epitome of the grumpy disciplinarian we all knew, strict but fair. I, too, tried to ensure my men and women wanted for nothing,

TV Series Gets To 'Heart' Of Policing

Police News – **December 1998**

This month Swasie recounts his pleasurable visit to the cast of 'Heartbeat' at the invitation of old friend Derek Fowlds. Being a TV police drama set in the '60s Swasie felt quite at home.......

"Of all the police series, I consider Yorkshire TV's Heartbeat to be most accurate..."

even if a few 'sirs' got upset!

I was made aware of the professionalism of the 'Heartbeat' team as they strove to create total realism. Scenes of 20 seconds duration were being filmed over and over again until the director was totally satisfied. Viewers would be amazed if they knew how much repetition goes into the most insignificant scene before it is deemed 'screen worthy'.

One small criticism though, I wish that PC Bradley, Jason

Swasie enjoys a joke with Bill Maynard on the set of 'Heartbeat'

Durr, would shed those high leg boots and crash helmet and revert back to the overcoat, police helmet and lightweight motor bike of his predecessor, PC Rowan, as played by Nick Berry. These

were a much more authentic image of those days.

I do, also, hope the writers continue these portrayals and do not let 'political correctness' creep in and destroy it.

Good luck to all at 'Heartbeat' - you portray the service in a good light, as it should be, and is. Our police service is the envy of the world, keep up the good work - we love you all.

left, Swasie and Derek Fowlds chat to a 'modern' customer of the 'real' village stores in Goathland right, Jason Durr came in for some lighthearted criticism from Swasie about his bike and his boots!

Swasie arrived at the lovely port of
Douglas on the Sea Cat Ferry whose
crew and passengers alike wished him
every success.

80

Isle of Man TT Mountain Circuit

20th September 1998

After contacting friends in the Isle of Man to 'sound them out' regarding an attempt on their famous TT course, Swasie was met with stony silence!

"Not surprisingly, there was complete disbelief at such an eccentric request...."

Not surprisingly, there was complete disbelief at such an eccentric and seemingly 'impossible' request.

Such a feat - travelling the gruelling 37¾ mile mountainous circuit in a standard wheelchair had never even been contemplated before in the history of the internationally famous event. Silence gradually gave way to polite scoffing at the thought of such an improbability.

Not to be deterred, though, Swasie told his sceptics that he had completed previously considered 'impossibilities'. There were his 41 mile Talacre

and 72 mile Anglesey 'jaunts'. It was respectfully pointed out to him, though, that this 'jaunt' would be totally different.

The course would be far too difficult for anyone to propel a 57lb wheelchair with his bare hands for such a distance. He was warned of the physically demanding terrain involved. Hills of 1 in 8 gradients, continual six-mile climbs, the daunting ascent up the side of Snaefell Mountain.

Features, it was pointed out, which taxed even the fittest of professional racers!

Nevertheless, Swasie was determined to have a go at the daunting 'challenge'. He would not be dissuaded and continued to seek permission to attempt the course. Eventually, his determination paid off and he was offered assistance from the island.

After listening to his pleas, a very sympathetic Anna Hemy of the Isle of Man Department of Tourism & Leisure accepted Swasie's credentials and assisted in this endeavour. She contacted the various authorities throughout the

It was respectfully pointed out that this would be totally different...

island and eventually permission was given for this, seemingly impossible, 'wheelchair marathon' to go ahead.

The Isle of Man Dept. of Tourism & Leisure assisted with Swasìe's and his carer's stay at the up-market Stakis Hotel, as well as arranging the travel to and from the island. This was far more than Swasie had ever encountered before.

Since he had started fundraising for the Cancer Fund all his previous stays had been paid for almost entirely out of his own pocket. Never seeking recompense, he ensured that every single penny donated went into the fund. Now, thanks to the Isle of Man Dept. of Tourism & Leisure and the Isle of Man Police and Fire Service, the

event was finally arranged to go ahead on Sunday 20th September 1998.

On the way to the island, crossing the Irish Sea from Liverpool, the captain of the Sea Cat ferry introduced Swasie to the passengers announcing his intentions over the public address system. Crew and passengers alike wished him every success in this seemingly 'crazy' endeavour and donated generously to the fund.

They duly arrived in the lovely port of Douglas and on that Saturday evening Swasie took to his comfortable bed in the plush Stakis Hotel. Lying there he began to recall the earlier comments of friends and wondered if this time he might have 'bitten off too

below, Swasie paused with Anna Hemy of the Tourism Department for photos before setting off

much'. But, no point worrying now, he thought, tomorrow is the day!

On a warm Sunday, as the sun rose over Douglas, Swasie was up early, his doubts of the previous evening dispelled in the bright morning sunlight. He tucked into a hearty breakfast - he was going to need all the fuel he could take on!

A large crowd of sightseers had gathered at the Grandstand overlooking the start of the famous TT circuit. As usual, publicity

"His doubts of the previous evening were dispelled in the bright morning sunlight..."

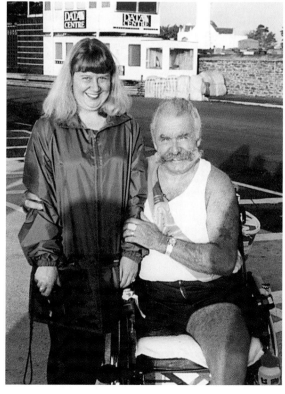

had preceded him ensuring a good send off. The Tourism Department's organisation was superb - fire engines, police officers and their dogs as well as other members of the island's emergency services assembled at the start and the media cameras rolled. A six foot three inch 'Viking' attended in full regalia holding his sword and shield aloft, dwarfing those he stood alongside.

Swasie was now anxious to get moving. Eventually, at 8.30am, he set off from Douglas into the unknown. Many, who stood witnessing this and knowing his intended route, privately considered this venture to be 'a bridge too far' - one that surely could not be completed.

They underestimated Swasie's determination, physical strength and stamina cultivated over the previous two years during which he had propelled himself and his 'tank' over massive distances.

right, at times, it was as though the roads went on and on up into the sky, a seemingly endless trek

However, this, in no way diminished the task ahead, and Swasie knew it.

Having taken advice from both the police and the Dept. of Tourism & Leisure Swasie decided to tackle the course in the opposite direction from the TT race so that he would face the tough mountain section early rather than later.

Leaving Douglas, its bay and harbour, Swasie swept out round Governor's Bridge, climbing through Cronk-ny-Mona and on to Brandish Corner and the famous Creg-ny-Baa. On past Kate's Cottage through Keppel Gate and still the climbing continued.

"The weight of the chair had started to tell quite early.."

After climbing continually for over an hour Swasie, himself, began to have doubts. He wondered if he had, in fact, underestimated the task ahead as he had thought the night before. These continuous steep and endless climbs were horrendous. The weight of the chair had, surprisingly, started to tell quite early with this continual climbing. Swasie was beginning to feel pangs of apprehension as the miles

Swasie soon left Douglas and the peace and calm of its harbour, right, far behind as he started out on this huge challenge...

83

were strenuously, but oh so slowly, completed. At times, it was as though the roads went on and on up into the sky, a seemingly endless upward trek - there was no respite.

Gritting his teeth in determination Swasie spoke to his beloved Marje, he told her he would complete the distance for her, no matter how long it took!

On through Windy Corner, the road signs and place names became a blur as he toiled ever onward. Gradually, the daily distances of twenty plus

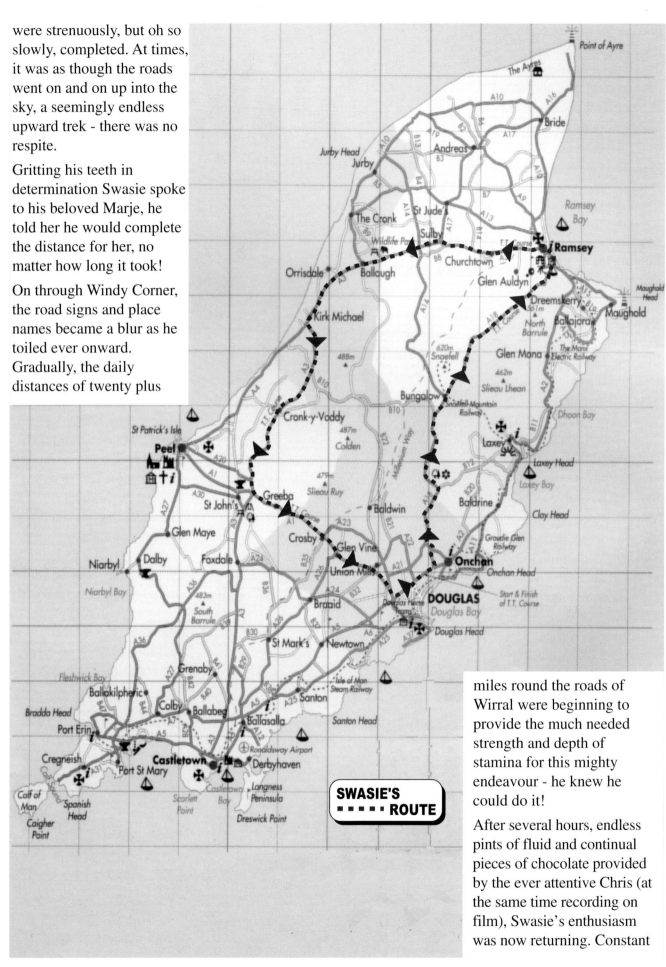

SWASIE'S
ROUTE

miles round the roads of Wirral were beginning to provide the much needed strength and depth of stamina for this mighty endeavour - he knew he could do it!

After several hours, endless pints of fluid and continual pieces of chocolate provided by the ever attentive Chris (at the same time recording on film), Swasie's enthusiasm was now returning. Constant

encouragement from Chris and the confidence-boosting presence of the police Range Rover as it monitored progress from a discreet distance behind, fuelled Swasie's determination more and more.

Motorists, ramblers, motorcyclists, residents and cyclists, all gave generously into his collecting 'bucket' to acknowledge the efforts of this lone pusher as he continued his seemingly relentless task. Swasie's determination kept him moving onward, at times pitifully slowly as the constant climb took its toll of his energy. Eventually, however, the plastic 'bucket' (a container with a slit in the top) hanging from the handle of the wheelchair became so full of coins that it had to be removed as the weight was affecting the progress of the climb.

The sun climbed high into a cloudless sky and beat down relentlessly forcing much needed fluid to perspire profusely from the gutsy trekker's body. Swasie's fluid intake could not keep up with his fluid outlet as he powered on incessantly - and there was still over 30 miles to go!

Swasie reached the famous Bungalow and he could see the daunting mass of Snaefell looming ahead. He

above, Swasie could see the daunting mass of Snaefell looming ahead. He moved on over the tracks of the Snaefell Mountain Railway

below, the going down was as hard as going up as his hands 'braked' the wheels to hold back the heavy chair

moved on over the tracks of the Snaefell Mountain Railway, as it crossed the road and wound its way up to the summit. Then it was onward and ever onward up this unforgiving mountain.

With huge relief he finally reached the highest point, around 1,400 feet on the side of Snaefell, with magnificent views across the Irish Sea. He paused for a while to take in the vista and gather his strength before moving on again - at least now there would be a long downhill section!

He passed the Graham Memorial, Stonebreaker's Cottage, through the East Mountain Gate, down the Mountain Mile and on to the Cutting - landmarks known so well to motor cycle racers for almost a century. At times, though, the going down was as hard as the going up as his hands desperately 'braked' the wheels to hold back the heavy chair. Then it was on down past the Guthrie Memorial to the 12 mile

> ## *The sun climbed high into the cloudless sky and beat down relentlessly...*

HAILWOOD'S HEIGHT

now on. Not literally, but that psychological barrier had been passed, the 19 mile point - he was now nearer the finish than the start!

The afternoon drew on as Ballaugh and Birkin's Bend were passed. Then it was through Kirk Michael, on the west side of the island, and onto part of the old short circuit, first used for racing in 1907. Baaregarroo, Handley's Corner and the oddly named Cronk-y-Voddy, gave way to Creg Willey's and Glen Helen. Then it was into Ballig Bridge and on to Ballacraine, where the old short course came up through St Johns from the beautiful port of Peel. He was now on the final 'leg'.

The afternoon gradually turned into early evening as he ploughed on through Greeba Bridge, past Greeba Castle and into Crosby. Only five miles to go! It seemed much easier now but the light was failing as this bizarre little convoy - Swasie's

point, and the delightful little port of Ramsey came into sight. Through the Gooseneck, past the Waterworks, round the Ramsey Hairpin and down into the town itself.

People sitting outside cafes and public houses left their tables to donate cash and pose for photographs alongside the wheelchair crusader as the little town's roads slowly passed by under his wheels and castors. From now on, though, coming out of Ramsey, he would be climbing again, not as hard as the first section up the

above, Swasie pauses to look down on the delightful little port of Ramsey as it came into sight

mountain, but, nevertheless as the day drew on, it sapped his stamina.

From Ramsey's Parliament Square he made his way slowly towards Schoolhouse Bend and then on to Glentramman and Kerroo Mooar. Through Sulby Bridge and Sulby Cross Roads he was approaching half way now - it would be 'downhill' from

" *...he was now nearer the finish than the start!*"

right, Swasie came down the famous Gooseneck bend into Ramsey somewhat slower than Mike Jeffries, left, went up it in the annual TT races

wheelchair followed by Chris's car and then the police Range Rover taking up the rear - slowly meandered on through Ballagarey and into Union Mills.

Eventually, darkness crept up on them and the small but bright flashing lights attached to Swasie's chair were switched on to illuminate his presence. Then it was down to Quarterbridge and round towards Douglas and the finish. Douglas would soon be in sight - well it would if it wasn't so dark! Then at mile 37 there was the

right, as the afternoon drew on Swasie came to the oddly named Cronk-y-Voddy 'driving with care'

infamous Bray Hill.

Now, the decision to tackle the course in the opposite direction hit back with its own 'sting in the tail'.

TT motorcyclists come DOWN Bray Hill picking up speed by taking advantage of this long incline from the start.

Slowly and painfully the 1 in 8 gradient, nearly a mile long, was climbed, sometimes just a yard at a time. Swasie was now totally exhausted and nearing collapse. Medics, concerned for his well-being offered to 'bring the line forward' to save him further pain. But he would hear none of it - he was within sight of his target. Determined as ever, he refused all assistance offered by concerned

onlookers and by, a now very concerned, Chris.

Head down, he quietly talked to his beloved Marje

below, the 1 in 8 gradient of Bray Hill, nearly a mile long, was climbed in the dark in the lights of the following Land Rover

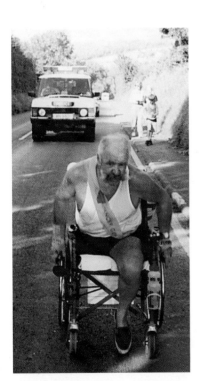

...it seemed much easier now, but the light was failing on this bizarre little convoy...

"...in front of the grandstand where he had started eleven and a half long hours earlier"

and with a final push he was there!

After what had seemed an eternity - 11 hours and 30 minutes of non-stop pushing - Swasie's piston-like arms had finally propelled him across the finishing line at mile 38. (Actually 37.8!) He was greeted by rapturous applause from the large crowd who had gathered to witness history being made - something they thought impossible.

The mighty 38 mile Isle of Man TT motorcycle racing mountain circuit had now been conquered by a one-legged man in a 57lb DHS wheelchair!

Swasie was back in Douglas in front of the grandstand where he had started some

eleven and a half long hours earlier. He had confounded his critics, the doubters, all those present. He had achieved what was considered by many to be physically impossible.

He was elated - but exhausted. He felt like crying, but he had done it, and he had done it for Marje. She had watched over him during those long hours of relentless pushing. This was, without doubt, his greatest achievement.

> "She had watched over him during those long hours..."

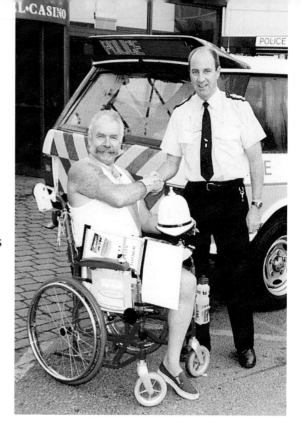

above, Swasie was presented with a 'white helmet' of the Manx Police as a memento of this quite unique event

During this exhausting journey the generous people of the island - residents, holidaymakers and tourists alike - had filled his bucket with cash which, when counted later, totalled an astonishing £670. Due to this outstanding success and the ensuing publicity, a further £400 was subsequently donated for this endeavour.

After a well-earned night's rest at the Stakis Hotel, Swasie was up early for a more leisurely tour of the island in the company of Sgt Peter Young of the Isle of Man Police Force. However, before setting out Swasie was presented with a distinctive 'white helmet' of the Manx Police as a memento of this quite unique event.

During a delightful day Swasie was taken south to

left, Swasie passed the beautiful Sulby Glen about halfway round the course but had no time to enjoy the scenery

Castletown and Port Erin and west to the delightful port of Peel, places off the motorcycle racing circuit. He also visited Laxey to see the famous waterwheel and saw some of the beautiful countryside which make this island such a popular destination for short breaks and holidays.

All too soon, however, the 'pleasure trip' was over and Swasie and Chris embarked

On his day of leisure Swasie was taken west to the port of Peel, above, and he also visited Laxey, right, to see the famous waterwheel

on the Sea Cat for the return journey to Liverpool. Again, as on the outward journey, the ferry's captain broadcast Swasie's presence, but this time was able to report the success of the mission. Swasie, again, was inundated with donations from both passengers and crew.

An added accolade is that

this Isle of Man 'feat' is being considered for inclusion in the Guiness Book of Records. Whether or not this feat gets into the book, it is doubtful if it will be accomplished again, let alone even tackled!

Swasie's time of 11 hours 30 minutes will probably stand, unchallenged, for ever!

left, Swasie with Sgt Sid Barry at Peel Cathedral, and right, he visited the Isle of Man Steam Railway which links Douglas and Port Erin

"*It is doubtful if it will ever be done again - Swasie's time of 11 hours 30 minutes will probably stand for ever!.....*"

Motorcycling History of the Isle of Man

The International Tourist Trophy Races

The world famous Isle of Man T. T. Motorcycle Races celebrated their 90th anniversary in 1997, having started in 1907.

But why was this tiny island in the middle of the Irish Sea chosen as the venue? To find the reason we have to go back to 1904.

That was the year the Manx Road Closing Act was passed by the Manx Parliament to enable the

"we have to go back to 1904 to find the reason"

"The winner's average speed was 38 mph, today it's over 120 mph..."

Gordon Bennett Motor Car Racing Trials to be held. In fact, the act was passed by both houses of the parliament and signed in the same day!

Moving on to 1907, motor cycling was becoming popular, particularly on the continent of Europe. The Auto Cycle Club, the forerunner of today's organisers, the Auto Cycle Union, wanted to hold a motorcycle race meeting in the British Isles. But, there was a problem, United Kingdom laws did not allow roads to be closed, and there was a strict speed limit on vehicles. So, remembering the 1904 Act, the club turned to the Isle of Man and the act was quickly amended to include motorcycles - and so the Tourist Trophy Races were born.

The course selected for that first race was the St Johns Course, or the Short Course, starting at St Johns, on to Ballacraine, then following the present course to Kirk Michael, then to Peel and back to St Johns, a distance of just under 16 miles. The

> ## it was felt that bikes would not be able to manage the climb up Snaefell

race was to be 10 laps, a distance of 158 miles, with a ten minute break halfway through.

The reason for the choice of this course was that it was felt the bikes would not be able to manage the 1400 foot climb up Snaefell Mountain which the cars used on the longer Mountain Course.

So, on 28th May 1907, 25 entrants divided into two classes, twins and singles, set off for the historic event. The winner's average speed was 38.22 mph, today it is

The Short Course, started at St Johns, went on to Ballacraine, then followed the present course to Kirk Michael, then to Peel, pictured above, and back to St Johns.

"over 40,000 fans travel to the island"

over 120 mph! The prize money then was £25, today it is over £13,000.

The 37.8 mile Mountain Course was first used in 1911, the races being the Senior, 500cc, and Junior, 350cc, over six laps, a distance of 226 miles.

In 1922 a third race, the Lightweight, 250cc, was added.

Today the T.T. has developed into a festival of motor sport, with over 40,000 fans travelling to the island for a fortnight of racing, including the T.T. races themselves, trials, moto-cross, sprints, grass track, sand racing, in fact every kind of motor cycling sport.

There are other motorcycle meetings held on the island. In July the 3 day Southern 100 meeting is held on the shorter Billown circuit and in August the 14 day Manx Grand Prix meeting also uses the famous T.T. mountain course.

Justifiably, in motorcycling circles, the Isle of Man is known as **"The Road Racing Capital of the World"**.

Swasie Turner ..... Off The Cuff

It appears there's a law for one – but ...?

It appears, with frustrating regularity, that if one is a member of that exclusive 'club', the Judiciary, it's okay to flout the laws of the land with impunity.

A number of recent cases seem to verify this. Cases where lawyers, especially judges, have been afforded what appears to be preferential treatment and have escaped the full 'wrath' of the law after committing criminal acts.

Wirral Champion – November 1998
Swasie, never afraid to speak his mind, wrote out strongly on a subject which caused him some considerable unease - judges judging themselves. He highlights two cases which make uncomfortable reading for those expecting to see justice done by the Judiciary!

The latest two appear, to put it mildly, to have been dealt with in a way which is nothing less than 'criminal' itself.

I refer to a lady judge in Wirral recently arrested for drink driving. She was found to be 'one and a half times over the legal limit'. Many police officers have had their careers terminated for the same, some even losing their freedom. However, did such treatment befall the most esteemed judge? Of course not!

Her punishment was just a fine and ... guess what? She is still allowed to sit on the bench in judgement of others. Mrs Lyn Hilton, founder of 'Mothers Against Drink Driving UK' angrily said, "*It really is one law for some, and another for the rest of us. She (the judge) put others' lives in her own hands and was lucky she didn't kill anyone.*" Mrs Hilton, who lost her 16 year old daughter to a drunken driver, went on, "*I am absolutely appalled on behalf of all the victims who*

> " *It really is one law for some, and another for the rest. The judge was lucky she didn't kill anyone* "

know only too well the scars left after child slaughter by drunk drivers."

I totally agree with you, Lyn.

Yet another blatant miscarriage of justice by the 'look after our own brigade' has reared its ugly head to upset the frustrated public once again.

Judge Richard Gee has been saved from the trauma and indignity of having to appear in the dock to face trial on an alleged £1 million mortgage fraud. Why? Because the Old Bailey was told he was so upset and depressed he might commit suicide! ... Tough! It was then cheekily stated that the 'sick' judge may well make a full recovery after this prospect has been eliminated.

The collapse of the case has left taxpayers with a £1 million legal aid bill! How many have unsuccessfully attempted to get legal aid and been refused for some pathetic reason? Answer - thousands of you. Yet, Judge Gee gets his legal aid

> ## the Old Bailey was told he was so upset and depressed that he might commit suicide!

granted, despite earning £86,700 per year as a judge, owning a £600,000 house in Belgravia, London, and residing with his very wealthy wife at her luxurious mansion in New York!

The scrapping of the case understandably caused anger and frustration among the investigating officers. The vain judge even insisted that those same officers should address him as 'Your Honour' as they investigated his dishonourable and criminal behaviour. An angry Scotland Yard Chief said, *"The public will be amazed that this man will not face a*

jury." I think that is putting it mildly. Words like 'furious' and 'incensed' spring to mind!

To put things in perspective, we have recently had a high profile case in Merseyside involving a police officer who received a lengthy prison sentence for corruption. I will not comment on the case, but I draw your attention to the comparison between a police officer (or anyone else for that matter) and a judge!

It was pointed out at the officer's trial that he had suffered 'severe depression' since the charges were brought, but in his case it fell on deaf ears. Surely "what's good for the goose...." It goes to show once again, that it's not *what* you know, it's *who* you know!

If it is deemed appropriate to satisfy justice and to act as a deterrent by making an example of errant police officers, then the same criterion should apply to wayward judges!

> ## A Scotland Yard Chief said, "The public will be amazed that this man will not face a jury

Epilogue

So where does Swasie go from here? Onward and ever onward appears to be the brief answer.

Shortly after completing the daunting Isle of Man TT Circuit he was climbing Liverpool's famous Liver Building, on the waterfront at the Pier Head, generously sponsored by the Rotary Club of Neston.

A further milestone was achieved on Sunday 28th February 1999 with the completion of a 'double marathon' from Christie's Hospital in Manchester to the Clatterbridge Oncology Centre on Wirral, a distance of 54 miles completed in just over 12 hours.

right, Liverpool's Liver Building was climbed in September 1998 left Swasie is a familiar figure on Wirral's roads stopping to talk to passers by

> ## "It was ironic that a charity supported by the London Marathon provides wheelchairs to youngsters!"

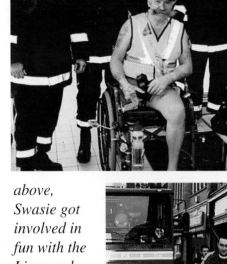

Next came a circuit of all the fire stations in Merseyside including 6 on the Wirral peninsula and 20 in Liverpool and its suburbs. Swasie dropped into each one for a chat and a collection to add to his ever growing fundraising total. Over a four day period this was a 'quadruple marathon' of over 110 miles.

A major set-back in early 1999, however, was the rejection of his application to take part in the internationally famous London Marathon. Considered unsuitable for the high speed 'professional athlete' wheelchair event and a 'possible danger' to competitors in the main event, this was a disappointment which raised many questions. It was also doubly ironic that one of the major official charities supported by the London Marathon in 1999 was one which provides wheelchairs to youngsters! Nevertheless, Swasie is determined to carry on and will apply again for future events.

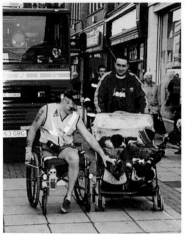

above, Swasie got involved in fun with the Liverpool Brigade on Red Nose Day

right, with young friends in Liverpool city centre

Since losing his leg in November 1996 Swasie has raised over £12,000 for the Clatterbridge Cancer Gene Appeal and in the process has travelled over 5,400 miles on the roads and by-ways of Britain in his trusty 'steed'.

Swasie was able to drop into 26 fire stations throughout Merseyside over a period of four days

lomax mobility

swasie got there
in his lomax chair

active daily living

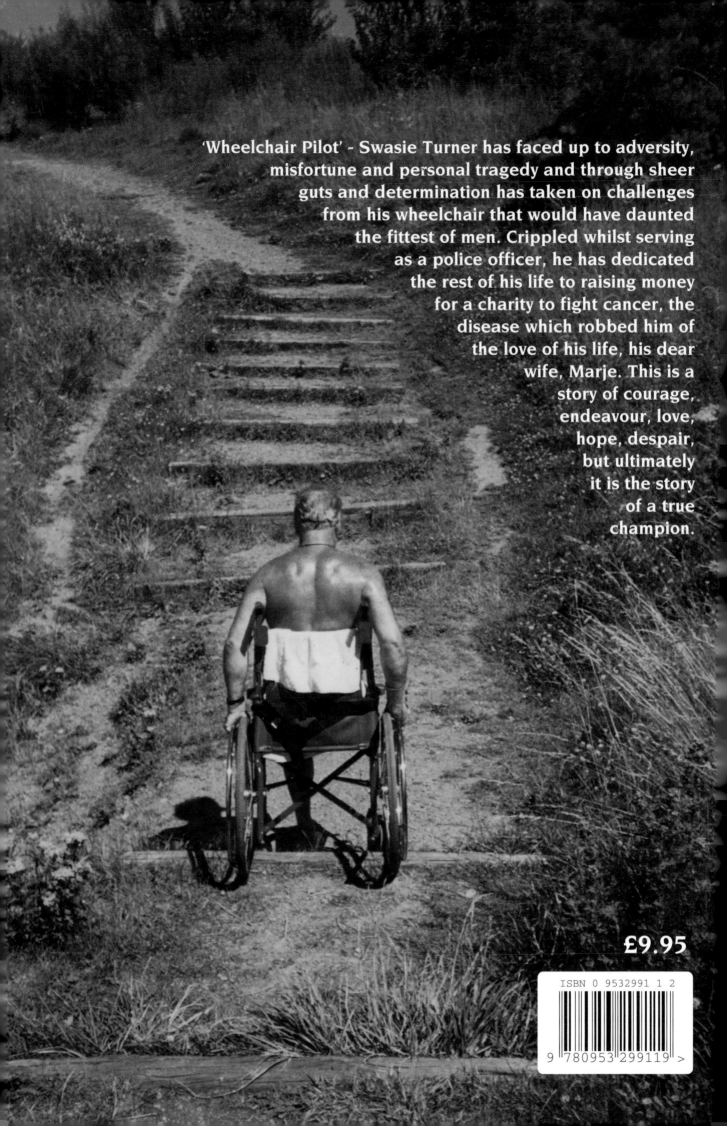

'Wheelchair Pilot' - Swasie Turner has faced up to adversity, misfortune and personal tragedy and through sheer guts and determination has taken on challenges from his wheelchair that would have daunted the fittest of men. Crippled whilst serving as a police officer, he has dedicated the rest of his life to raising money for a charity to fight cancer, the disease which robbed him of the love of his life, his dear wife, Marje. This is a story of courage, endeavour, love, hope, despair, but ultimately it is the story of a true champion.

£9.95

ISBN 0 9532991 1 2

9 780953 299119

Key Stage 2

Reading Comprehension Workbook

SATs Skills

Reading
Comprehension
Workbook

- Supports the
  National Curriculum

- Pull-out answer
  section

- Progress charts
  to track learning

10–11+ years
Stretch

10–11 years

9–10 years

8–9 years

Introduction

The **Bond SATs Skills** range has been designed to develop core skills for success in Key Stage 2 National Curriculum (SATs) tests, the 11+ and the Common Entrance tests. *Bond SATs Skills Reading Comprehension Workbook Stretch for 10–11 years* focuses on extending essential comprehension skills needed to excel in these key tests.

What does this book contain?

- **10 units of activities** – covering the comprehension element of the National Curriculum, providing comprehensive preparation for SATs, the 11+ and Common Entrance tests.

- **Progress chart** – this is a visual and motivating way for children to track their learning, found on page 48.

- **Scoring** – each page allows children to capture their score in the activities to see how they're doing.

- **Answers** – located in an easily-removed central pull-out section.

- **List of key terms** – key terms and phrases that children will need to be familiar with are in bold text throughout the book, and defined in a Key Terms section at the end of the book.

How can you use this book?

This book can be used at home, school and by tutors to:

- Provide regular comprehension practice in bite-sized chunks

- Highlight strengths and weaknesses

- Set homework

- Set timed practice tests to build exam skills for formal testing.

Don't forget the website!

Visit **www.bond11plus.co.uk** for lots of advice, information and suggestions on everything to do with Bond and helping children to do their best.